PRESENTATION TIPS AND TECHNIQUES

Mike Levy

 Panic-free presentations

 Ready-made ideas that cut preparation time

 Visual techniques that will double your impact

 A powerhouse of expert tricks of the trade

Wyvern Crest
Publications

Published by

Wyvern Crest Publications
A Division of
Wyvern Crest Limited
Wyvern House
6 The Business Park
Ely
Cambs
CB7 4JW
01353 665522

First published in 1997

British Library Cataloguing in Publication Data.
A catalogue record for this book is available from the British Library.

ISBN 1 899206 10 8

Typeset by PanTek Arts, Maidstone, Kent.
Printed by Bell and Bain Limited, Glasgow.

Contents

Acknowledgements   ix
How the Book was created   x
Introduction   xi

Part One: ZAP! - Creating knock-out visual aids

1 Which visual aid? – choose one that will shout your message

Visual aids – do I need to use them at all?   3
– turn a dry monologue into a diverse and stimulating event

Which visual aids are available?   6
– low-tech and high-tech – they all add atmosphere

Which visual aids work best?   7
– think carefully what you want to say

What is the best means of delivery?   8
– for real impact you must enjoy using the aid

Flipcharts   10
– beautifully simple and spontaneous

The overhead projector (OHP)   12
– immediacy, impact, integration and interest – all in one

Whiteboards   16
– a striking background with the big plus of very little to go wrong

Slide projection   19
– a clear, sharp colourful medium – excellent for larger presentations

Video   20
– the most powerful medium

Which visual aid should I use?   22
– follow the checklist chart and select the media to suit your need

2 OHP transparencies
– tips, tricks and techniques to present a punchy image

Get to know your equipment 23
– *just 4 items to get you up and running*

Transparencies 23
– *the dos and don'ts of film, photocopiers and printers*

What about pens and markers? 27
– *types, tips and highlighters that enliven and excite*

How do I prepare a transparency? 27
– *by hand or computer, 7 golden rules for your text*

How do I make the text effective? 34
– *using words that will grab your audience*

How much of the transparency should I use? 35
– *bright and busy but not too crowded*

I'm not a designer – how do I create effective transparencies? 37
– *use pictures, keep words to a minimum and add colour*

What is the best way to present numbers? 43
– *line graphs, bar charts and pie charts for a graphic approach*

Accessories for producing more professional transparencies 49
– *graphics, dry transfer lettering, stencils and specialist tools*

How do I use overlays? 51
– *for revealing information step by step, a simple but impressive technique*

Creating an OHP presentation using your computer 53
– *for a really slick presentation, modern technology offers endless possibilities*

How should I look after my transparencies? 57
– *if you need to use them again store them carefully*

Taking care of the projector 59
– *5 don'ts to give your machine a longer life*

How do I prepare the room for an OHP presentation? 59
– *5 room layouts to choose from for the optimum impact*

What preparation do I need to do? 65
– *19 essential checks to get the room, equipment and materials just right*

What is the best way to use the overhead projector? 66
– *9 nitty gritty dos and don'ts for proficient presenting with a projector*

Should I use the reveal technique? 68
– *will it distract and could an overlay be used instead?*

3 Flipcharts
– be your own creative designer and raise the applause

What kind of room is best?   73
– keep it small and informal – too big and it won't be seen

Get to know your equipment   74
– 4 items to get you going

Flipchart pads   74
– the good, the bad and the indifferent

How do I design an effective flipchart sheet?   76
– key rules to keep it clear, simple and visible

How do I use the reveal technique?   87
– 2 methods – one of them will suit your purpose

Flipchart presentations with a difference   90
– 5 ideas for turning a low-tech medium into a high profile presentation

Troubleshooting   91
– common problems to be prepared for

Checklist – preparing to give a flipchart presentation   91
– 19 checks about position, preparation and practice

4 Whiteboards
– add a dash of spice to the white space

Get to know your equipment   93
*– make sure you use the right marker pens and have proper cleaning
   fluid to hand*

How can I keep my whiteboard information?   95
– electronic boards will give you a print out

Pepping up the whiteboard   96
– lettering, colour and keeping your writing straight

How do I prepare for a whiteboard presentation?   97
– the room and visibility

Checklist for a whiteboard presentation   98
– 6 essential checks to get it right

5 35mm slides
– put yourself in the limelight with bold, sharp images

Get to know your equipment   99
– only 3 items that you need

Projectors   99
– the essentials and the extras to make it that bit easier for you

Screens   101
– 7 types to choose from – with their pros and cons

Creating exciting visuals   102
– 6 golden rules and colour combinations that work best

How do I produce my own slides?   103
– this is easy but for close-ups you need to employ specialist techniques

How do I look after my slides?   103
– 5 key points to remember

How do I give a slide presentation?   104
– preparation, rehearsal, lighting and best practice techniques

Checklist – tips for a skilful slide presentation   105
– 8 essential points to help you present like a pro

6 Video presentations
– sound and motion for a super-strong message

Get to know your equipment   107
– the products and control facilities that you need at your fingertips

Preparation before using a video   108
– 4 musts for a smooth presentation

Video dos and don'ts   108
– the annoying irritations to avoid

Positioning the video   109
– the best place so everyone can see

How do I make the most of a video presentation?   110
– don't treat it like a film – think what the clip shows

Checklist – preparing to use a video   111
– 6 important points for technical reassurance

Part Two: Presentation know-how – ensuring everything is all right on the night

7 Three weeks to go
– plenty of time, but time to make a start

What message do I want to deliver?   116
– pare your presentation down to the core

Who is my audience?   117
– the more you know about them the better you will be

What do they already know?   117
– pitch it right and put yourself into their shoes

How large is the audience?   118
– *the size will determine which visual aids you should use*

Where will the presentation take place?   120
– *the venue can determine the success of your presentation*

How long will it last?   120
– *5 golden rules on timing*

How do I start?   121
– *get it off to a good beginning*

What result do I want?   121
– *think about what you want and what the audience wants*

8 Two weeks to go
– structure, story and variety

Gather your materials together   125
– *planning the framework and structure*

Deciding what to use   127
– *cut out anything that is there just for the ride*

Look for a story   128
– *tips for turning facts and figures into a fresh invigorating experience*

Should I use a script?   129
– *keep it natural and learn the art of making it look spontaneous*

Keep it short and simple   130
– *the best advice – no one ever complained about a presentation being too short*

Look for ways of adding variety   130
– *18 tips and tricks for adding variety to your verbal and visual presentation*

How what you say interacts with your visual aids   131
– *topical tips for keeping the interaction flowing*

9 One week to go
– time to rehearse and gain feedback

Rehearsals   134
– *test, familiarise and practise to overcome any anxiety*

Feedback   135
– *get a practice audience to mark your presentation against this 16 point checklist*

The dress rehearsal   136
– *combine text and visuals for the best run through*

10   On the day
– making sure it all goes to plan

Avoid last minute emergencies   137
– keep your cool

Checklist – just before you go on   138
– 4 key points to check before you begin

What do I do if a visual aid goes wrong?   138
– a 4 point emergency plan

30 minutes before   139
– some relaxation and voice preparation techniques

11   Making the presentation
– keeping on an even keel and handling hiccups

The first few minutes   141
– what to do and how to do it

How do I keep the presentation smooth?   142
– techniques for keeping it flowing

How do I deal with interruptions?   143
– how to keep your cool and handle them with good humour

Dynamic delivery   144
– adding variety, dealing with hesitation and mannerism, words to avoid,

How do I come to a strong finish?   146
– look for the high note that will lift the audience

Making a presentation in a hurry   146
– an 8 point plan for a cool, calm and collected delivery

Appendix I: Rapid reference presentation planner   149
A fast track flow chart for planning every presentation

Appendix II: Presentation problem buster   151
Cut through over 70 problems you may have to face

Index   157

Free Special Report   162

Acknowledgements

Special thanks to the many experienced presenters who were consulted for their practical advice including: Brian Gillard, Training Manager of Dow Stoker; Brian Clark of Film Sales Ltd; David Martin of the Buddenbrook Consultancy; Catherine de Salvo of Fenman Training and Cristina Stuart of SpeakEasy Training. If you would like further information on training courses in presentation skills please contact: Cristina Stuart at SpeakEasy Training, 309 Ballards Lane, London, N12 8NE tel. 0181 446 0797; David Martin is the author of *How to be a great communicator* (Pitman) 1994; Fenman Training supply a range of videos, training kits and other materials for professional trainers (tel. 01353 665533).

A special thankyou to all the companies who supplied information and some of the illustrations for the book including: Acco-Rexel Ltd, Associated Visual Products (AVP), Nobo Visual Aids Ltd, Schwan Stabilo Ltd, Staedtler (UK) Limited, 3M United Kingdom PLC, Pelltech Ltd, Quartet Manufacturing Company.

How the Book was created

Many different people and sources were consulted in the creation of this book. They include expert trainers, managers and professional presenters, all of whom regularly use these techniques. Without exception they generously gave their time to explain the tricks of the trade, which they have perfected by trial and error, enabling you to take the short-cut to putting them into practice immediately.

A host of helpful suggestions and advice was supplied by the companies that manufacture and distribute the presentation equipment discussed in this book and they also took time to explain the intricacies of their products.

Numerous authoritative books, pamphlets, catalogues and other materials were also scoured to check data and facts. This wealth of knowledge has been expertly distilled to give you the best possible pack of presentation tips, techniques and tricks for you to use in your next presentation.

The burden of pulling all this information together fell heavily on the shoulders of Mike Levy, and the greatest thanks are due to him for swiftly bringing the book to fruition.

Introduction

ARE YOU PANICKED BY PRESENTATIONS?

On the Richter Scale of stressful situations giving a presentation comes close to the top for many of us. We all want to be able to present like a pro – as if it is the most natural thing in the world. By following the advice in this book you will be able to step confidently into the spotlight and know that you will make a polished, professional presentation – one that will stand out from the crowd and instantly win the audience over to your side.

Seeing is believing

If you ask people what they liked about a particular presentation invariably it is not what they heard or what the speaker said – it is all about what they saw. More than 50 per cent of people's impressions about a presentation is to do with visual impact. That means for your presentation to be memorable you have to make a strong impact with visuals that really sparkle.

Get your visuals right and you are half way there

Which is exactly what this book will do for you. The verbal aspect of your presentation is still important (you can't expect a presentation to stand or fall by your visual aids) but if you get your visuals right you are more than half way to winning the battle. But we don't just cover the visual aspects of creating visual aids – how you use them is equally important. If you follow the advice in this book you will be able to interact with the aids confidently and creatively.

HOW THIS BOOK IS PUT TOGETHER

The book is divided into two parts. Part One covers all the information that you need to create and deliver knock-out visual aids, whether they are OHP transparencies, flipcharts, whiteboards, 35mm slides or video presentations. Part Two gives you a three week run down to your presentation giving you a step by step plan to getting it right every time. In the appendices you will find a bonus pack of information to make your presentation that much easier. This includes:

✓ a rapid reference flowchart for planning your presentation;
✓ a presentation problem buster solving over 70 tricky situations you may have to face.

The goldmine within

In addition the book is packed with a goldmine of advice to make your presentation that bit special including:

 Hot tips! – using just one will make your presentation special;

 Tricks of the trade – what the pros do;

 Presenters' prompts – personal advice from the experts (people pay hundreds of pounds to hear them);

 Graphics – ideas for instant images you can add to your transparencies / flipcharts and make your presentation sparkle;

 Golden rules – that will help you get it right every time;

Illustrations – showing you how to do it (and how not to);

Checklists – to make your presentation perfect;

Time-saving tips – short cuts to preparing your presentation;

Warnings – helping you to avoid those danger spots.

You know already you can give a good presentation. With the help of this guide you will be able to turn a *good* presentation into a *great* presentation!

Part One

Creating knock-out visual aids

Which visual aid? –

choose one that will shout your message

 "First impressions really do count. If you don't capture your audience in the first few seconds you will have lost them."
Catherine de Salvo, Fenman Training

A visual aid helps to communicate information and ideas. Because its medium is visual, the aid has immediate impact in providing detail and direction for your audience.

VISUAL AIDS – DO I NEED TO USE THEM AT ALL?

You could present your material as a lecture or a speech. Giving a prepared talk at least means that you are not at the mercy of a piece of technology. There's just you and the audience. So why not use just words alone?

A visual aid is just that: it helps you do something with your presentation that your voice alone could not do. Visual aids should always be seen as the servant of your presentation, never its master; they should never take anything away from the presenter. Only as a last resort should aids be used as a prop to support the nervous presenter – even then however good the aid, it will not cover up a presentation that is poorly planned or verbally inadequate.

✓ Right – choose the ideas you want to present first and then the visual aids which will best illustrate them.
✗ Wrong – choose your theme to suit the visual aids you have.

What we see has a much more immediate impact than what we hear. Research has shown that over 50 per cent of the impact in a presentation is down to what the audience sees, both in terms of you as a presenter and the visual aids you use. Under 40 per cent of the impact comes from the voice and less than 10 per cent is in the content, or the actual words you choose. So it is vitally important that you get the visual aspect right. One of the drawbacks of visual aids is that they can distract an audience from what you are saying. The more 'arty' the visual, the more distracting it can be.

Only consider using visual aids when they have a clear purpose and can do things which words alone could not do.

A visual aid is useful to make the structure of your presentation more interesting to the audience: it provides a welcome break from listening and gives the presenter a good reason for movement. The visual aid helps to make a presentation much more interesting and varied for the spectator.

Visual aids are often a better way of presenting complex information, especially information which deals with inter-relationships between points, processes, procedures, summaries, technical drawings, statistical data, maps and other largely visual information.

To give your presentation a strong focus, distil all your ideas down into one short sentence. That sentence is the message of your presentation. Keep it in mind as you prepare, deliver and end your presentation.

The main strength of a visual aid should be its clarity – it means that there is less chance of misinterpretation than with a purely verbal presentation.

A well-designed visual aid also transmits to your audience that you consider them to be important enough to have gone to a great deal of trouble.

Information visually presented is:

* often more stimulating than the spoken word;

* easier for an audience to understand and therefore saves time;

* usually remembered for a much longer time.

when to ...

"Using visual aids is vital when I want to show how things work; the relationships between A, B and C and to present items such as sales trends and profit forecasts."
Managing Director of a wholesale clothing firm

The pitfalls of visual aids

However, visual aids are not without their problems. If used for the wrong reasons or used badly they can:

- **distract the audience** – visual aids should not upstage the speaker. Aim to get the visual aids to reflect your message. If it is a fairly sober one, you shouldn't use too much razzamatazz in designing your visual;

- **appear boring and diminish your impact** – many a good verbal presentation has been spoilt by dull, over-wordy or unreadable visuals;

- **interrupt your flow** – always remember that visual aids are for the audience and should not be used as your notes;

- **appear badly designed** – this can antagonise an otherwise supportive audience;

- **let you down if you don't use the technology correctly** – it is easy to put slides in upside down, or for an overhead projector bulb to blow, or a pen to run out. While this may be amusing for the audience it will be embarrassing for you and, more importantly, it will obstruct your message.

You stand up to deliver your presentation, you switch on the projector and nothing happens. The bulb has blown. What do you do? Do not replace it yourself. Calmly ask the event organisers to fix it. Divert attention away from the projector by moving into the middle of your audience and start an open-ended dialogue with them. For example, break the ice by asking people what they hope to learn from the day, or what difficulties they have experienced so far with X, or one of the other "w" words to open them up: why?, where?, when?.

"To break the ice in a small business presentation you must get the audience to tune in with you. If you can give a benefit to your audience as to why they should listen to you then you will capture their attention. For example, you might say 'what I have to say today will save you two hours of your time next week'."
Cristina Stuart, SpeakEasy Training

Grab your audience's attention at the start. If you lose them at the beginning you will find it difficult to hold their attention until the end.

"The way to tackle nerves before a presentation is to prepare properly. Practise out aloud beforehand in order to become familiar with the sound of your voice and the flow of the words. This practice will also give you a rough idea of the timing of the presentation."
Cristina Stuart, SpeakEasy Training

WHICH VISUAL AIDS ARE AVAILABLE?

There are many types of visual aid on the market, ranging from very simple ones to those with a good deal of high-tech complexity.

Simple-to-use visual aids:

- flipcharts;
- whiteboards;
- chalkboards;
- product displays.

Low-tech visual aids:

- slide projectors using 35mm transparencies;
- magnetic boards;
- overhead projectors using acetate and other film material;
- video playback machines;
- 8mm and 16mm film.

High-tech visual aids:

- computer graphics linked to a large screen by LCD (Liquid Crystal Display) panel;
- combined video, sound and graphics players.

The visual aids most commonly used in commercial presentations are the 35mm slide and the overhead projector transparency. These are excellent for formal, preplanned presentations. For informal, interactive discussions, most experienced presenters would use a flipchart for both audience and speaker to add ideas as they arise. Of course, your presentation may well consist of both formal and interactive sections: you may wish to use slides or transparencies to present the essentials of your argument and then utilise the flipchart for noting ideas coming from the audience.

We only have a limited time available ...

We want to win and we will win ...

This book focuses on the most commonly used visual aids:

* flipcharts;

* whiteboards;

* overhead projector transparencies;

* 35mm slides;

* video;

* computer-enhanced graphics.

Handling hecklers. It is rare to have hecklers at presentations but this is what you should do. Invite them up to the front and let them have their say. They won't feel half so secure as they did shouting from the safety of the back, and nine times out of ten, they will bottle out. If they do come up, give them ten minutes to have their say and then continue with your presentation.

WHICH VISUAL AIDS WORK BEST?

In choosing which type of visual aid to help support your presentation, first think about what you want it to do. Each type has its own particular strengths and weaknesses. You may of course be limited in your choice of visual aid by the budget, the size and shape of room, the size of the audience and so on. But if you are given some flexibility, how do you choose which one to use? The answer depends in part on what type of information you wish to present.

The type of information that you give may involve:

* **defining** – giving the exact meaning of a particular term or piece of jargon;

* **explaining** – expanding information to make your meaning absolutely clear;

* **reinforcing** – strengthening a point so your audience fully believes in what you say or remembers that point more than anything else when they leave;

* **clarifying** – making sure your audience really understands what you have to say;

* **summarising** – providing pointers of what has been covered so far;

* **creating an atmosphere** – so the mood and tone are memorable for the participants.

Once you have a clear idea of what you want to say in your presentation, you can start to plan how you will say it: using graphics, illustrations, statistics, flow charts, bar and pie charts, bullet points... You will come across stacks of examples in this book that can easily be borrowed and incorporated into your own presentation, whatever the occasion.

You may wish to develop an idea which gradually builds into a larger picture – the overhead projector transparency is very good to use in an overlay technique where one illustration is superimposed on another to create a final picture. We will see how this can be done later in the book.

"With a large audience of 50 to 100 people I would not encourage lots of participation because there is a danger you will go way off-beam with the timescale for the presentation."
Catherine de Salvo, Fenman Training

WHAT IS THE BEST MEANS OF DELIVERY?

In order to make the most out of your visual aids during a presentation, you should ask yourself the following questions:

☐ Is the slide or other visual aid appropriate to my ideas?

☐ Is this the best way of getting my ideas across?

☐ Does it make my ideas easier to follow?

☐ Am I confident that I can use the visual aid effectively and without hesitation?

One of the most important points about visual aids in a presentation is that you feel, and are seen to be, comfortable using them. An effective visual must flow on seamlessly from what you are saying – it must not disturb the flow of your presentation.

The more you can enjoy using the aid, the more relaxed the audience will be. The simple rule here is that if you cannot get used to using visual aids, or are bad at designing simple but effective visuals, do without them. Play to your strengths and never use a visual just because it is the expected thing to do.

"I used to use overhead transparencies that had been prepared for me by an excellent cartoonist. They were funny and very clever but it was not me. All they seemed to do was stop the audience in its tracks and make them think, 'that cartoonist chap is clever, pity about the presenter'."
A personnel manager

Your visual aids should look as professional as possible. This means:

● they should look good and seem to be produced with some care;

● they should be clearly readable;

● each visual should have a clear house style – keep colours, designs, typefaces and font sizes consistent.

Although we will deal with the techniques of using each type of visual aid, here are some general guidelines for getting the most from all kinds. Use the points as a checklist before making any kind of presentation using visual aids.

CHECKLIST – Getting the most from your visuals

☐ Always rehearse or practise using the aids, especially if they are new to you.

☐ Try to ensure a fairly even space between each visual and your talk. In general do not show more than two visuals without speaking. If you choose to use visual aids, make sure that they are used for at least 25 per cent of your time. There is nothing more distracting for the audience than having, say, an OHP that is hardly ever switched on.

☐ Check that everything is in working order before giving the presentation and before the audience arrives.

☐ Keep your visuals as simple as possible – it is very rare to find a visual with too little information on it, much more common to find ones that have far too many words or diagrams on them.

☐ Give the audience a chance to take in the visual – remember that unlike you, they haven't seen this before. Make sure the key message of the visual gets across and is understood, but do not waste time by simply reading it out word for word.

☐ Do not let the impact and dramatic tension of your presentation evaporate while switching on the next visual or writing something on a board or chart.

☐ Remove the visual as soon as you have finished with it – never leave it hanging there while you have moved on to the next point.

☐ Maintain eye contact with the audience as often as you can – do not keep looking down at your notes or at the screen.

☐ If you want to use notes, hand them out at the end of the presentation but not at the beginning. The activity of handing them out causes a distraction: the audience's attention is taken off you as they try to absorb the information in front of them and you lose that all-important eye contact.

Once you have prepared the structure of your presentation, reduce your notes by half. This will stop your presentation from becoming too long and help you to focus on only the key messages.

"I never use a script or long-winded notes. It's too tempting to bury your head in them and lose contact with the audience. If I must use prompts, I write the key points on small cards that I can hold up or better still, pencil in little crib notes on the cardboard margin of the transparency or flipchart."

A professional presenter

FLIPCHARTS

A flipchart is probably the most common and the cheapest visual aid and yet it can also be one of the most effective forms of presentation. A flipchart is really only a large tear-off pad, usually mounted on an easel.

When is the best time to use a flipchart?

Here are some guidelines that will help you decide.

Guidelines

Flipcharts are especially useful in situations where you want to encourage audience participation, either in the form of ideas elicited from individuals or a report back from a group. Here your flipchart will be blank and you can either write down the ideas coming from the group or get someone from the group to write down their own ideas.

Flipcharts are especially useful when:

- you are leading an open-ended discussion or a brainstorming session;
- you want to create a spontaneous atmosphere;
- you want to get the group to write down their own ideas;
- you elicit ideas and thoughts from the group and you want to record them for further discussion;
- there are several ideas that you want to keep in people's minds.

Where there are several key points that you want to keep in front of the group, pin or stick each completed chart around the room. You can use small tacks if there is a suitable pinboard available, or double-sided tape or Blu-tack for posting the charts on the surrounding walls.

Flipcharts can be used for proactive group sessions

If you wish to present points already prepared in advance, you can use pre-drawn charts. Use these when:

● you have some key learning points to make in a particular order;

● you want to give instructions for a role play or other participative exercise;

● you would like to show a sophisticated graphic which would be difficult to draw on the spot;

● you wish to use an idea or thought as a stimulus for group discussion – as an example your opening chart may contain one statement such as:

How can we boost our profits by 25 per cent in two years?

Use strong bold colours such as blue and black for lettering on OHPs and flipcharts. Weak colours such as yellow and orange will not show up well.

"Flipcharts are very portable and can be prepared in advance. It's also a blessing not to have to rely on electrical supplies or any other technology that may let you down on the day. I find them particularly invaluable in group discussions – people actually like seeing their own ideas up there in print. It's also a good idea to let the group come to the front and add in their own points to the chart."
Marketing manager of a food distribution company

When not to use a flipchart

Think twice about using flipcharts when:

● **The group is large (more than approximately 30 people).** Flipcharts are relatively small and can be difficult to see clearly at the back of a large room. They are also not very high, so that unless the room has raked seating the chart may be obscured by people in front.

● **It is important that the results of the discussion are copied.** A flipchart page is too large for most photocopiers, so unless you have the time to copy the pages on to a smaller format, you should consider other visual aids (such as overhead projector transparencies).

● **The quality of design and presentation must be high (at say a product launch or press conference).** Unless professionally produced in advance, it is difficult to make a flipchart look really good. Much depends on your handwriting, spelling, ability to draw and so on.

● **You do not want to turn your back on the audience.** As you write down points on the chart, it is unavoidable to turn away from the audience. This can be overcome, of course, where the chart is pre-drawn or when you expect the audience to do most of the writing.

Time-saving tip

Prepare a handout in advance with all the key points covered. Leave some spaces for further ideas. These can be filled in at the end of the session acting as a summary of the the main points written down on the charts you have used.

"It is very important to break up your presentation if it is a long one and vary the pace. If you have got a small group, get them to do something; this keeps them involved and awake and encourages them to contribute. If you are talking to a large group you need to vary the presentation and employ other devices: show them a short video clip or hand something round. I think it is good to engage people's five senses. If you have got something for them to smell, let them smell it, or if you have got something for them to taste, let them taste it."

Catherine de Salvo, Fenman Training

THE OVERHEAD PROJECTOR (OHP)

An overhead projector is a piece of equipment that allows you to draw, write or use ready-made images that are enlarged and projected onto a screen that stands above and behind the speaker. (see Figure 1.1).

Do you want to draw an image onto an OHP but are worried about getting the image right first time? First draw the image onto a backing sheet with a grid and then trace the image onto the transparency.

The special advantages of the OHP are:

● You present in normal light – there is no need to darken the room or use blackouts.

● You can maintain a central position in the room by placing the projection screen to your right (or left if you are left-handed) (see Figure 1.2).

● You can face the audience throughout the presentation. Maintaining eye contact with them helps you to gauge their reaction to your presentation and keeps their attention focused on you.

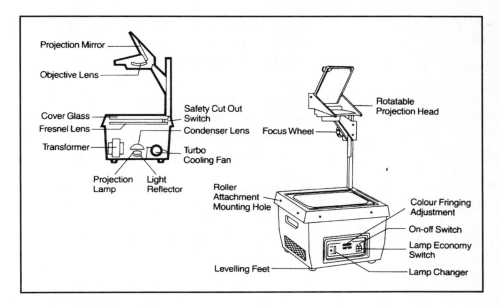

Figure 1.1 A standard overhead projector
*Get to know where all the switches are and what each one does. It is surprising
how many presenters stand up to give a presentation and have no idea where even
the on/off switch is located. Note the other features you may need to use such as
the focus wheel, colour fringing adjustment, levelling feet and how to attach a roller
for continuous film.*

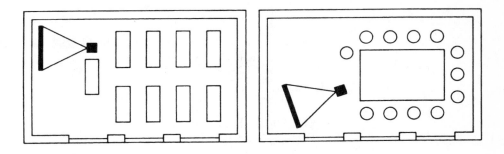

Figure 1.2 Maintaining a central position by keeping the screen to the
side of you
*It is good for you and for the audience if you can maintain a central position
throughout your presentation. Keeping the screen to the side of you will also help
you to avoid getting in the way of the light beam and the screen, causing an
obstruction for your audience.*

Always tell your audience where you are going and how you are going to get
there. Give them clear signposts or landmarks to watch out for in the
presentation. Summarise what you have to say frequently.

- You can switch the image on and off as often you wish – this can be used for very precise timing. For example, Figure 1.3 shows a transparency containing part of an idea.

Figure 1.3 could be shown as a summary of the points covered so far. Switch off the OHP, discuss other values and then, as a summary, place the next transparency on the light table (see Figure 1.4) and switch on to show all the ideas.

- You can modify or add to charts and illustrations as you speak to help give immediacy and impact to your presentation.

- You can use your PC or other computer to create graphics and text.

Company Values

- customer
- professionalism
- profitability
- respect
- continuous improvement

Figure 1.3 Summary of points covered so far
Use OHPs to time carefully what you present and when you present it. It is dangerous to bombard your audience with too much information all at once.

Company Values

- customer
- professionalism
- profitability
- respect
- continuous improvement

plus...

- teamwork
- safety
- excellence

Figure 1.4 The full summary
Having delivered a partial summary you may want to add other ideas and then remind your audience of what the complete picture looks like.

In short the advantages of the OHP can be summarised by the four 'I's of Immediacy, Impact, Integration, Interest.

IMMEDIACY	the visual aids are ready at precisely the moment they are needed.
IMPACT	large bright visuals demand attention, lead the audience's eye and help them to memorise points.
INTEGRATION	the presentation is live and under the presenter's control. The method is flexible enough to adapt to the audience's needs.
INTEREST	the use of effective visual aids increases the audience's motivation and helps retain their attention.

Source: Staedtler *Project Yourself* Workshop Notes

The key point here is that the OHP keeps you in control.

Express negatives positively. "Because we achieved only 80 per cent of the target, we have had to abandon the idea of taking on an extra marketing manager" is far better than "Because we did not hit the target, we cannot hire an extra marketing manager".

Warning

The OHP's job is to magnify the image on the transparency. Any mistake or imperfection will therefore be greatly exaggerated. Make sure that the acetate is clean and that any spelling mistakes are corrected.

OHPs – the disadvantages

* Using them well takes practice.

* The equipment can be bulky and difficult to move around.

* Materials are quite expensive.

* There is no movement or sound.

* They may be inappropriate for very large audiences – text can be difficult to read from the back of a big hall.

To generate interest in your audience from the start, offer them a promise (but make sure it can be delivered). For example, "This presentation will take 30 minutes. In half an hour you will be able to go away with five new ideas that can be used instantly to increase your sales".

If you have never used an overhead projector before you will be surprised by its versatility and ease of use. Used in the right way, it is also a very powerful visual aid: bold, clear and effective. Prepared transparencies that look very professional are simple to produce (see Figure 1.5).

You also have the option of writing out your message as the presentation proceeds (see Figure 1.6).

"Be careful about telling jokes against groups of people unless you are part of that group. It may be appropriate for a woman to tell a joke about women but it could be received very differently from a man." *Cristina Stuart, SpeakEasy Training.*

WHITEBOARDS

Many of the features and characteristics of the flipchart can be found in the whiteboard. Indeed many flipchart easels incorporate a whiteboard surface. This is very useful as the portability of the flipchart can be used here to good effect. This section tells you which to choose, how to get the most out of whiteboards and when to use them.

When is the best time to use a whiteboard?

Like flipcharts, whiteboards are especially useful when:

- you are leading an open-ended discussion or a brainstorming session;

- you want to create a spontaneous atmosphere;

- you elicit ideas and thoughts from the group and you want to record them for further discussion;

- you want to provide main headings as the basis for discussion;

- you want to show a linear development of thought on a large board (see Figure 1.7).

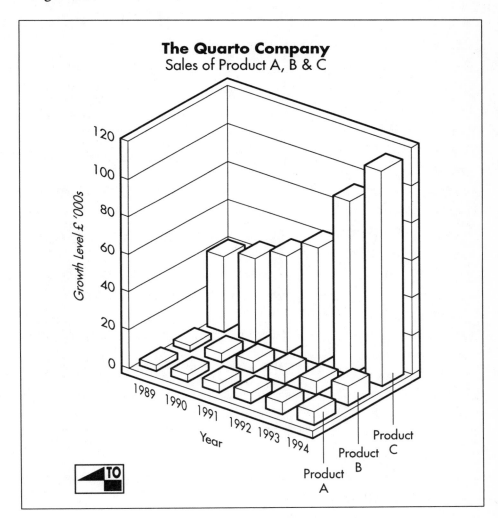

Figure 1.5 Prepared transparencies that look professional are simple to produce

To create a really powerful visual aid try using a 3D effect. It will make your visual stand out from those around you. But take care not to cram more information than can be absorbed by your audience onto one visual.

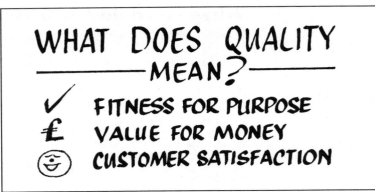

Figure 1.6 Write out the key points as the presentation proceeds
Keep it fresh and spontaneous. Don't make the mistake of trying to write onto a loose transparency on top of an OHP projector – you will find it difficult to keep the transparency still. Instead, use a film that is fixed onto a roller on the side of the projector which will keep it steady and help you to maintain the flow. Note how it is possible to produce even simple graphic images to reinforce the message.

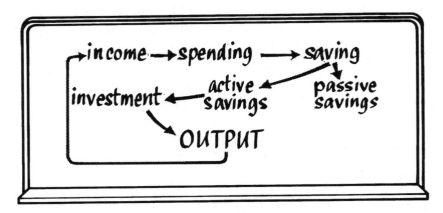

Figure 1.7 Using a whiteboard display to illustrate a linear development of thought
Break your ideas down into concise statements and then build them up to demonstrate how your ideas link together to show the relationships between them.

A presentation involving just a speaker delivering a monologue to the audience can be very dry. Break up the presentation by getting your audience to actively participate in what you are saying. Here are five useful ways:

● Ask the participants questions.

● Ask the participants to complete gaps.

● Invite each participant to contribute one idea.

● Ask them to give you their experience of a situation.

● Make them complete a quiz, test or competition.

Why are whiteboards so useful?

Whiteboards share many of the advantages of flipcharts:

* there is little to go wrong;

* they don't rely on electric power.

In addition whiteboards enjoy the advantage over blackboards that they are cleaner and free of chalk dust.

Warning

If you are using a computer or a video recorder, avoid using a chalkboard – the dust can do a great deal of damage. Use a whiteboard instead.

Whiteboards provide a clean, brilliant white background which makes your text or diagram very easy to see. They can also be used as a screen onto which slides could be projected. If you do this, check out the room lighting first; the whiteboard surface often reflects light back.

Made a mistake? You can easily correct a whiteboard presentation by simply wiping any contents away with a dry cloth. This is perhaps their biggest advantage over other visual aids.

Like the flipchart, whiteboards are ideal for informal, interactive presentations where ideas are elicited from the audience. However, unlike flipcharts where sheets can be posted around the room, the amount of writing space on a whiteboard is limited.

Consider using a whiteboard in conjunction with a flipchart. The board can be used for main headings, the chart for the audience to add their own ideas.

SLIDE PROJECTION

Most people are familiar with slide projectors. These use the small card-mounted 35mm photographic film normally professionally prepared (but not always so). Black and white or colour slides can be projected on to a large screen. The images projected can be extremely clear and sharp with excellent colour contrast. Slides can give a professional look to any presentation.

Avoid using "I", "me" and "my" in your presentations – they will not help your audience to empathise with you. Focus instead on "we", "you" and "us" – win your audience over to your side.

The pros and cons of using slides

The pros:

- The presentation can feel more formal.

- They give excellent colour definition.

- They are particularly good for larger audiences.

- They are relatively cheap to produce.

- They are durable (if handled properly).

The cons:

- They cannot be written on so your presentation lacks spontaneity.

- There is a danger of mishap – such as slides falling out of order.

- It is easy to put them into the projector the wrong way round or upside down.

- You may have less control in how they are produced.

- They take longer to produce than OHPs.

- You lose eye contact with the audience.

- Rooms need to be darkened.

But all of the pitfalls in giving a slide presentation can be avoided by careful preparation.

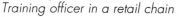 "If you put up an OHP transparency the wrong way round, no one seems to bother but get a slide upside down or in the wrong order and people seem to think it's hilarious. It's much easier to make a fool of yourself with a slide presentation."
Training officer in a retail chain

VIDEO

These days it is easy to buy or hire videotaped programmes that have been specially made for management or other business presentation purposes. If you have the budget you may choose to show your own specially commissioned video.

Using a video programme as part of your presentation can add a lively touch to the session, bring a point to life and make a powerful impact in a way that only film and television can do. And it can provide a welcome break from speaking. However, there are problems in using this visual aid, as you will see. Like any other visual aid it must support, not replace, your presentation. Use the video too much and it can do more harm than good.

Go out with a bang, not a whimper; your audience will remember you and your presentation far better.

Film or video?

Video has largely replaced the use of 8mm or 16mm film. In some ways this is a pity: the clarity of film is usually greater than that of video, and you could use a much bigger screen. Apart from lack of availability, however, film involved large, often noisy projectors that were difficult to load and often broke down; it also meant that the room had to be darkened.

Using video

Videos are easy to use, and most people these days are well used to playing, pausing, rewinding, fast forwarding and so on.

The right way to use video

The best time to use a video is when you want to give the audience a break from your voice (though do not introduce it as a more attractive alternative to you). It is also very useful for giving background information, helping an audience visualise a location, setting a mood, presenting role play and case study material and showing data, statistics or other information where movement and sound are important. Video is often used to show people giving their views and offering opinions. This can be very useful, but see the discussion below of things to avoid.

Video is different from other media

The video is such an all-embracing mix of sound, vision and movement that it is tempting to see it as almost an alternative to the live presentation. This would be a mistake. Although, unlike the other media, video is very familiar to everyone, its use in the presentation should be very carefully handled. The main reason is loss of control. More than any other type of visual aid, except perhaps film, you can be tempted to hand over the session to others.

Unlike other visual aids, it is quite difficult to interact with a video without breaking the flow or distracting the audience. Video is a very powerful medium and people tend to remember what they have seen – make sure that it is used with discretion.

 "One of the affects of adrenalin is that it speeds up your perception of time so what might seem a terribly long pause to you is only a split second for your audience."
　　　　　　　　　　　Cristina Stuart, SpeakEasy Training

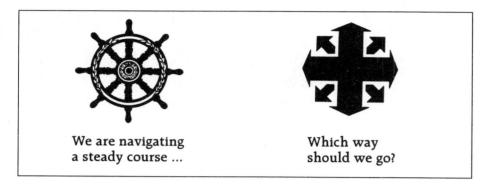

We are navigating a steady course ...

Which way should we go?

WHICH VISUAL AID SHOULD I USE?

Once you know what information you wish to impart and how to do this, you can consider the visual aid which best serves your purpose. Here are a few useful suggestions that should help you decide but don't treat them as hard and fast rules. Only your own preferences and experience will tell you which are the most suitable visual aids for you.

TABLE 1.1 CHECKLIST – Selecting your media

Your circumstances	35mm slides	OHP	Flip chart	White board	Video	Computer enhanced graphics
Large audience	✓	✓				✓
Small audience		✓	✓	✓		
Pictures to be shown	✓				✓	
Overlays to show how an idea develops		✓				✓
Limited budget		✓	✓	✓		
Eliciting ideas from the audience		✓	✓	✓		
Drawing flowcharts which are added to as you present		✓	✓	✓		
Showing material produced on a computer		✓				✓
Summarising points made by the audience		✓	✓	✓		
High quality graphics	✓	✓			✓	✓
Providing case studies to promote discussion	✓				✓	
Bringing your ideas to life					✓	✓

OHP transparencies –

tips, tricks and techniques to present a punchy image

 *"Check the OHP projector before you go on – I once had to contend with a glass top that had chip marks in it. Everyone thought it was my transparencies that were damaged rather than the machine which needed repairing!"*
David Martin, Buddenbrook Consultancy

GET TO KNOW YOUR EQUIPMENT

To run an OHP session you need:

- the projector;
- transparencies;
- a screen;
- marker pens.

 *"I always put the OHPs on myself and issue handouts personally. I think it is very important because deliberate movement helps to keep the audience's interest. If you deliver a static presentation from a lectern the audience will quickly tire of looking at you. It helps to bring the presentation more to life. You do have to be careful though to avoid irritating repetitive movements otherwise the audience may start to look at these and not at you!"*
David Martin, Buddenbrook Consultancy

TRANSPARENCIES

The best OHP projector is only as good as your transparencies. This is the basis of your presentation – the medium in which you will present text or images. The way an OHP works is that a transparent film made from PVC, acetate or polyester is placed over the light source (on a standard OHP model) and anything that is marked on the film is enlarged and projected onto the screen. The film is an optically clear material able to show a written or drawn message or set of images.

Transparencies are easy and convenient to prepare because you work in the familiar and compact A4 size. Enlargement is done by the projector.

The way you produce your transparency will decide what type of film you buy. There are different types of film for different purposes. It is very important to use the right kind of film.

A simple guide to OHP transparencies

A word about definitions:

- **film** – the clear medium on to which text or graphics are written or copied. This is what you buy from your stationers.

- **transparencies** – the finished article ready to use on an OHP.

- **acetate** – one of several types of material from which the film is made.

If you want to write directly on the film use a transparency made from *acetate* or *hard PVC* (a lower-cost version of acetate suitable only for one-time use).

If you want to produce a transparency via a photocopier or printed out from a computer use a transparency made from *polyester*.

Never use a transparency made from acetate in a photocopier, laser or other type of printer. It could seriously damage your machine.

It is a common misconception that all transparencies for OHPs are called "acetates". This is not the case: acetate is only one kind of film. If in doubt check with your office supplies dealer that you are using the right type of film.

Don't put in a visual aid just to fill a gap. Ask yourself:

- does it explain?
- does it make it easier to understand?
- does it spice up the presentation?

Film rolls

In addition to the flat sheet transparencies, most suppliers produce rolls of film that are usually ready-wound on to specially designed spindles to fit scroll attachments mounted on the side of the projector. The film can then be wound on, presenting a fresh sheet each time. This technique is better for spontaneous presentations than for prepared sessions. The film roll saves you having to find new sheets from the pad.

Only use film rolls when you expect a lively, interactive session with ideas flowing quickly, and when a flipchart is unavailable. It is quicker to roll on a fresh transparency than discard the old sheet and replace it from a box.

Using a photocopier to produce a transparency

Effective transparencies can be made by using standard office photocopiers. You can produce superb transparencies including text, charts, technical drawings, graphics, text. It's as easy as making any photocopy.

Remember that an audience's attention is high at the beginning, gradually declines over the next 20 minutes and then rises quite steeply at the end of the presentation. Make sure the message you want them to remember is delivered clearly at the beginning and at the end of your presentation.

"The photocopier is brilliant for copying black and white text and graphics. Just put the film into the feed tray, place your original in the usual place and press the 'copy' button. The machine will copy your original on to the transparency in the usual way. The results are usually excellent."

Coloured film
"For showing black and white text, I use a coloured film for better visual impact and to give my audience a break from the glaringly white screen. Yellow, light blue or orange are good. The coloured film usually has a deeper coloured margin which frames the image in a pleasing way."

Not this way
"Never photocopy whole paragraphs or worse, pages of text – it is almost unreadable on screen. If you must do this, use handout notes."

Using your computer to generate OHP slides

Computers are increasingly being used to create quality presentations using both text and graphics.

There are different ways of printing out the material originated by your computer:

- dot matrix printer;
- inkjet and bubblejet printer;
- laser printer;
- pen plotter;
- thermal transfer printer.

Always use OHP film specially produced for each type of printer. Using the wrong kind of film can seriously damage your printer.

You can do very simple things such as print a page of text generated from your word processor, or data off a page from the spreadsheet or database.

Dot matrix

Dot matrix printers represent one of the oldest printing technologies for computers. There is a potential problem with them in that the transfer system is from inked ribbons to paper or specially coated film. This means that the colour contrast may be lower or there may be a problem in producing translucent images that project well. Colours may appear somewhat washed out, but you can still produce good quality graphics.

Use specialist film such as that produced, for example, by Film Sales, Staedtler, Nobo or Schwan Stabilo.

If you are producing black images on a dot matrix printer, Film Sales recommends that you print the output onto paper then photocopy those images onto Copystat film using any plain paper copier. Paper prints may be translated into colour transparencies by using CLC film on any colour laser copier.

Inkjet and bubblejet

Inkjet and bubblejet printers, such as the Hewlett-Packard Deskjet series, are becoming very popular with computer users. They are currently cheaper than laser printers (although the margin is rapidly narrowing) and yet the quality of output is almost as good. The one slight drawback is that the inks take longer to dry than other methods and transparencies should be handled with care. Take them out of the printer and leave them to dry for at least five minutes.

Make sure you only use film specially designed for inkjets.

Laser

Laser printers create exceptionally sharp text which is comparable with the most professional offset printing technology. Both inkjet and laser printers can be bought with a colour printing capacity, although the latter is still expensive.

Pen plotter

You can also produce more sophisticated transparencies by using special presentation software or generate a complex technical drawing using a plotter system. Pen plotters have been around a long time and they can produce very good transparencies. There is a good clean image and the film is crystal clear. The chief problem with plotters is that they are very slow, especially where you want to fill in bar charts with colour (it can take an hour or more for one copy!).

Thermal transfer

You can produce really high quality graphics using a thermal transfer printer. Here coloured waxes are transferred from an ink ribbon to the film. This process is particularly good for producing precise and brilliantly coloured images. The colour contrast using thermal printers is better than on inkjets – the yellows are more vivid and black shading is much more pure. Until recently thermal printers were outside the price range of most people, but since the advent of small desktop printers such as the Star SJ 144, thermal printing is becoming much more popular.

You don't need a colour photocopier or printer to add colour to your presentation. Take your black and white masters to a high street colour copying shop and ask them to add colour to pie chart segments, flow chart boxes or other illustrations.

 "Don't overload your audience with text on an OHP. Stick to one key point. If you have several points to make put up separate transparencies."

Catherine de Salvo, Fenman Training

WHAT ABOUT PENS AND MARKERS?

If you are going to write directly onto the transparency using suitable write-on film, make sure that you use the correct markers. There are many brands on the market but basically it comes down to a choice between two types: permanent markers, and non-permanent markers which are water soluble. Even permanent marker images can be removed with alcohol-based solutions or special correction pens, but for transparencies that you want to add to, amend or erase, use water-soluble pens.

Non-permanent markers

When you want to wipe off the image quickly and simply using a damp cloth, choose from the pens listed in Table 2.1.

TABLE 2.1 Non-permanent OHP markers

Brand of marker	Tip widths	Colours (up to)
Schwan Stabilo water soluble	4	8
Papermate non-permanent	2	6
Lumocolor non-permanent	5	8
Nobo water-based	3	8
Edding non-permanent	4	8

You should use a permanent marker if write-on transparencies have to be protected from accidental erasure. These pens are ideal to use on write-on film when you want to use the film repeatedly. (See Table 2.2.)

TABLE 2.2 Permanent OHP markers

Brand of marker	Tip widths	Colours (up to)
Schwan Stabilo permanent	4	8
Papermate permanent	2	6
Lumocolor permanent	5	8
Nobo permanent	3	8
Edding permanent	4	8

Although called "permanent" markers, the ink from these pens can actually be removed by using spirit-based solutions or by using a special correction pen – do not despair if you make a mistake!

You can erase "permanent" ink using such items as the Edding 160 correction pen, the Nobo OHP Eraser, or the Lumocolor EX-319 correction pen.

To use a correction pen, simply make a few strokes over the area you wish to erase and wipe over with a tissue.

When to use different tip widths

* Use fine-tipped markers for drawings where detail and fine lines are needed.

* Use medium-tipped markers where your audience may be sitting quite far back.

* Use broad-tipped markers for headlining text.

* Use extra-broad markers for bold headings or filling in large areas.

Three absolute musts before your OHP presentation. Check you know where:

* the on/off switch is;

* the focus knob is;

* the replacement bulb is (and how to replace it).

Highlighters

Very effective use can be made of special OHP highlighters which can enliven a black and white transparency or highlight particular features of the text during the presentation. These highlighters usually come in bright fluorescent colours. As an example, the Schwan Stabilo Projection Highlighter 730 and the Lumocolor AV Highlighter for film are both available in six colours.

Use highlighter on the reverse side of the film to avoid smudging.

 "I use cardboard mounts for transparencies. It keeps them in better shape and they are easier to place on the projector."
Cristina Stuart, SpeakEasy Training

HOW DO I PREPARE A TRANSPARENCY?

In advance:
- by hand;

- using photocopied images and text;

- using computer-generated text and graphics.

During the presentation:
- by hand using the transparency as if it were a notepad;

- adding to pre-prepared transparencies;

- laying a new transparency over an existing one to build up a picture, a diagram or a flow chart.

Tips for preparing an OHP transparency by hand

With a little planning, it is quite simple to produce transparencies that are effective and impressive. If you are going to write them yourself use a lined or grid backing sheet. You can buy these when your acetates are bought as a pad. The lines or grids will help keep your handwriting straight and legible, and you could also use the grids to mark out and design any illustrations.

You may want to draw the outline of the illustration in pencil directly on to the backing sheet first. Then once you are satisfied with the drawing, you can lay the transparency over the backing sheet and trace over the illustration using an OHP marker.

Tracing a drawing may be especially useful when you are using permanent marker pens for a transparency that you wish to keep.

 Amaze your colleagues with the power of your memory, jot detailed facts and figures down on the margin of an OHP transparency card mount or frame.

Remember only to use transparency that is specially designed for writing on – acetate or hard PVC film is appropriate.

If you are going to overlay several sheets to build up a picture, use acetate film as this is more robust than PVC-based film.

You may wonder which
way you should turn ...

We need to focus on
finding a solution ...

1. If you are underlining words or drawing lines with a ruler, use a very fine-tipped marker. This will prevent the ink bleeding under the edge of the ruler.

2. Avoid colours that are too weak for lettering: yellow and orange are examples.

3. Keep your words large enough to be seen. Make sure that each letter is at least 8mm in height, bigger if the audience is large (see Figure 2.1).

DISTANCE FROM PROJECTOR SCREEN	MINIMUM LETTERING SIZE
Up to 10 metres	**5 mm**
10 – 15 metres	**10 mm**
15 – 20 metres	**15 mm**

Figure 2.1 The further away from the screen, the larger the letter size and the thicker the pen stroke

Watch the size of your letters. If your audience is up to 10 metres away the height of your letters will need to be at least 5mm. If they are 15 to 20 metres away then the height will need to increase to at least 15mm.

Source: Staedtler, OHP Handbook, p. 17

4. Use the landscape format (lengthways) rather than the portrait shape. The latter often seems too cramped and there is a danger of losing the top and bottom of each slide. The landscape transparency is much better suited to the typical OHP screen. (See Figure 2.2.)

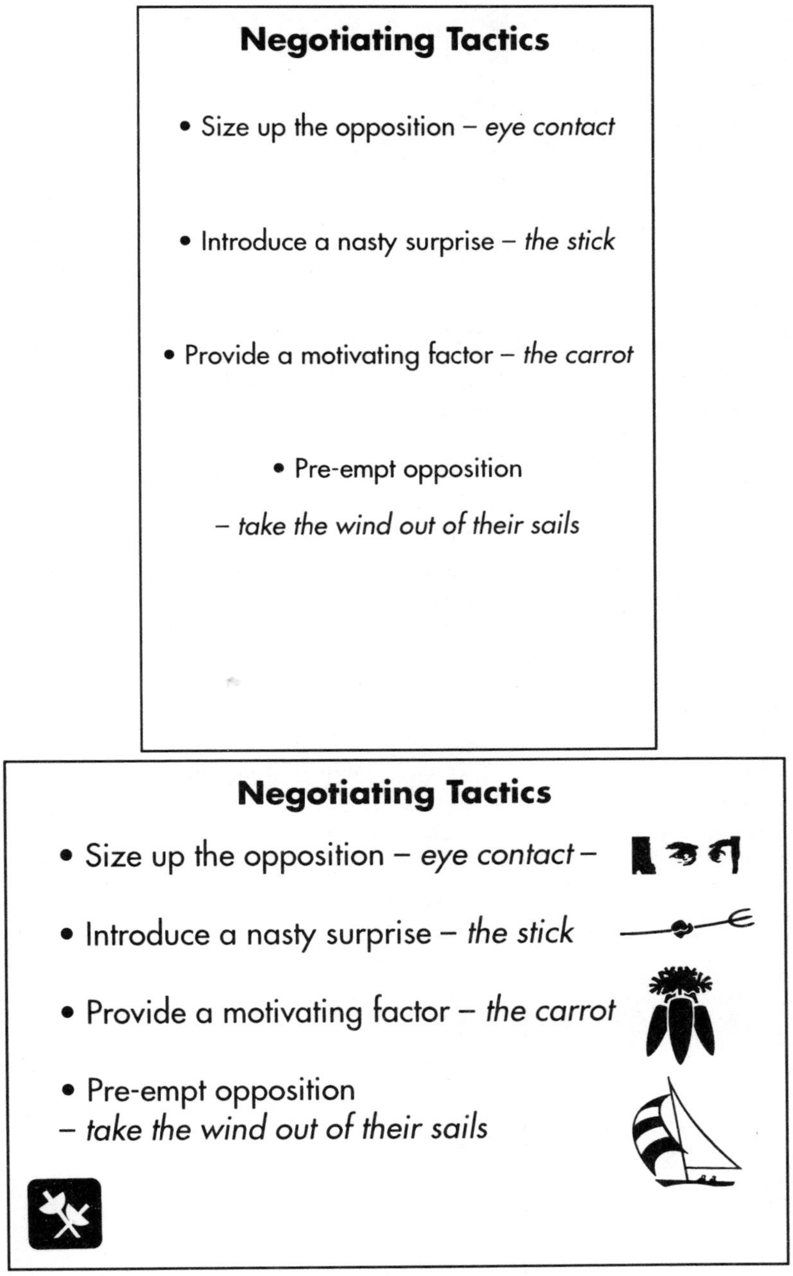

Negotiating Tactics

- Size up the opposition – *eye contact*

- Introduce a nasty surprise – *the stick*

- Provide a motivating factor – *the carrot*

- Pre-empt opposition
  – take the wind out of their sails

Negotiating Tactics

- Size up the opposition – *eye contact* –

- Introduce a nasty surprise – *the stick*

- Provide a motivating factor – *the carrot*

- Pre-empt opposition
  – take the wind out of their sails

Figure 2.2 Landscape and portrait compared
Using a portrait format restricts the number of words you can use per line. If you want to fit more words per line a landscape format will appear less cramped and there is less chance that words will get lost off the top or bottom of the transparency. You will also have more space for graphics.

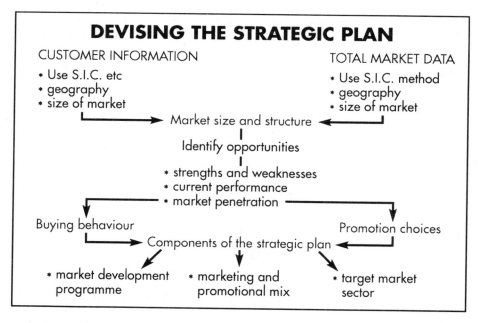

Figure 2.3 Not too many words on each line
Even on a landscape format you have to be careful not to put too many words on one line. The more words you have the less the impact will be and the more cramped it will appear. Stick to no more than seven words per line; the fewer the words the stronger the impact.

5. Limit the number of words per line. As a general rule of thumb, make sure that there are no more than 7 words to a line (see Figure 2.3).

6. Limit the number of lines per page. The OHP transparency in Figure 2.4a has too many. As a general rule there should be no more than 10 lines (and ideally no more than 7) to a page. (See Figure 2.4b.)

DEVISING THE STRATEGIC PLAN

CUSTOMER INFORMATION   TOTAL MARKET DATA

* Use S.I.C. etc   * Use S.I.C. method
* geography   * geography
* size of market   * size of market

Market size and structure

Identify opportunities

* strengths and weaknesses
* current performance
* market penetration

Buying behaviour   Promotion choices

Components of the strategic plan

* market development   * marketing and   * target market
  programme   promotional mix   sector

Figure 2.4a This OHP has too many lines
This presenter has crowded too much information onto the page.

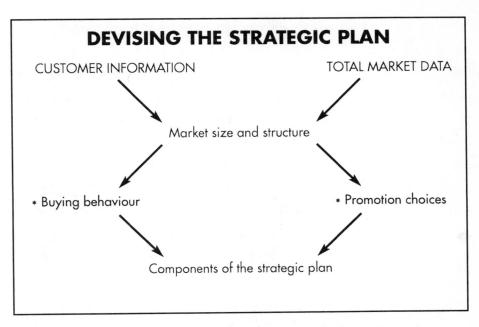

Figure 2.4b A less crowded page which is easier to understand
By reducing the number of sub-headings it is not only easier on the eye for your audience but is also easier for them to take in the message.

7. Avoid fancy lettering and handwriting that may have character in normal correspondence but are illegible in a presentation. Using both upper and lower case lettering will look more natural and less formal.

Use lower case rather than all capitals, it is more restful on the eye.

TOO MUCH USE OF CAPITALS IS
NOT ONLY WEARISOME BUT
IT BECOMES MORE DIFFICULT
TO EMPHASISE PARTICULAR WORDS
OR PHRASES. IT IS MUCH BETTER TO USE
CAPITALS SPARINGLY.

Additional guidelines for typed text

1. If you are using text that has been typed using a wordprocessor or typewriter, the lettering may well be too small. Use the enlarging facility on the photocopier to increase the size of the lettering and then copy this on to a suitable transparency. You can also use this technique for increasing the line spacing.
2. Choose sans serif fonts (typefaces) such as Helvetica and Univers – they are simple and unfussy. Serif and ornate fonts are not so difficult to read in printed text but are not at all clear on a screen.

3. Similar guidelines apply regarding the size of the text to those given for handwriting.

18 point (5mm) should be your minimum size – it may be too small to be seen more than 10 metres away.

28 point (8mm) is about right for most uses.

36 point (10mm) is good for main headings.

"I always give notes out at the beginning and leave a wide righthand margin on them for the audience to add their own comments. I don't put everything I say in the notes but deliberately leave specific points out. I issue these other points as handouts. This serves two purposes – it helps reinforce the point with the audience and gives me the opportunity to move amongst the audience building a rapport with them."

David Martin, Buddenbrook Consultancy

HOW DO I MAKE THE TEXT EFFECTIVE?

How can you make an OHP effective even if it consists mainly of text? Follow the checklist below.

CHECKLIST – Making the text effective

☐ Grab attention with the title or opening text. A question can be quite effective if it is one that the audience would actually ask themselves. For example, if you were introducing a new ice cream:

"What's so good about Polar Ices?"

☐ Use nouns or active verbs to begin the line – they also attract attention. For example:
* tastes natural;
* stays soft even in the freezer;
* reduces shelf space.

☐ Then use nouns to provide detail:
* **colour** – fresh and natural;
* **texture** – smooth but not runny;
* **packaging** – bright and attractive;
* **message** – a naturally pure and healthy product;
  – fun to eat;
  – a summery experience.

If your OHP appears on the screen as a strange wedge shape (the keystone effect), adjust the screen so it is 90° to the light beam.

 "I would always use an OHP projector that has a spare bulb in it."
Catherine de Salvo, Fenman Training

HOW MUCH OF THE TRANSPARENCY SHOULD I USE?

What is important here is balance and visibility. You don't want to leave too much white space because this looks distracting and can be rather glaring (see Figure 2.5).

The Customer is King

Figure 2.5 Too much white space
Too few words on a transparency can create a stark and cold impression on your audience. To soften the glare, consider reversing the letters out of a black solid box or print on to a colour tinted transparency.

There is so much white space here that the message looks too stark, too isolated and unfriendly – plus there is an awful lot of glare to contend with.

If the message is very short, consider brightening up the page with an illustration or graphic, as in Figure 2.6.

Figure 2.6 Brighten up the message with a graphic
Using a graphic image will not only help brighten up your transparency but it will also help your audience retain the message you are trying to put across far more than if you use words alone. Whenever appropriate, liven up your transparency with a graphic image, but don't crowd it with too many of them.

Here are some useful rules for keeping the transparency busy but not overcrowded:

1. Give preference to the upper two thirds of the transparency (see Figure 2.7). The bottom part could be used for less important information such as logos, titles, keys and so on. Keep important text and key diagrams in the upper two-thirds.
2. Leave a margin of at least 1.5 to 2 cm all around the edge – it can be quite attractive to draw this border in.

Watch out that your transparencies do not contain too much white space – it is glaring on the eye. A colour-tinted transparency will help to soften the glare.

"Eye contact is essential. I achieve this not by staring into the eyes of the audience which can be off-putting for them but by looking up and sweeping or sliding my eyes periodically over them. This makes my audience look at me – eye contact is maintained without causing anyone any embarrassment."
David Martin, Buddenbrook Consultancy

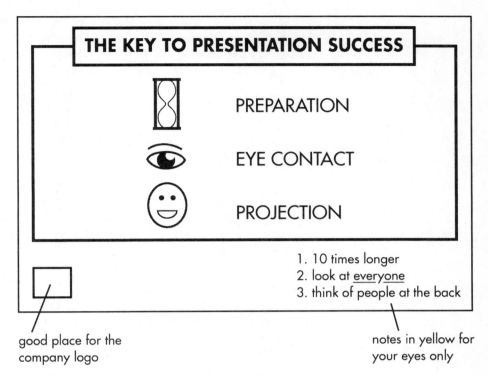

good place for the
company logo

notes in yellow for
your eyes only

Figure 2.7 Keep to the upper part of the transparency
Your audience will find it easier to absorb information if it appears on the top two-thirds of the transparency. However careful you may be to keep all the sightlines clear and remove all the obvious obstructions there will always be a minority of people for whom part of the screen will be obscured – perhaps by a fellow member of the audience. You can also write notes on yellow at the bottom of the transparency. These will not be visible to your audience – only to you.

I'M NOT A DESIGNER – HOW DO I CREATE EFFECTIVE TRANSPARENCIES?

Your OHP transparency should always be:

- easy on the eye;
- simple to understand and easily absorbed by your audience;
- easy to read even at the back of the room;
- interesting to look at.

How can you achieve these goals?

- by using clear and unfussy lettering of the right height;
- by making sure the transparency is uncluttered;
- by careful use of colour;
- by using illustrations.

"When I design a transparency, I write down the message I want to give, then cut the number of words by half without losing the meaning or clarity – the fewer the number of words, the more impact your slide will have."

An experienced accountancy trainer

Add colour to your presentation by copying your OHP masters onto a colour-tinted transparency.

Using colour

Coloured marker pens are one way of breathing life into your transparencies if you do not have access to a colour printer or copier. There are some key rules, however, that should be remembered:

Key rules

1. Don't go overboard with colour – use it wisely and sparingly.
2. Don't use more than four colours – your transparency can easily become garish.
3. Red and/or orange will bring lettering or graphics "forward" – make them appear to stand out.
4. Blue will make images appear to recede.
5. Use strong contrasts for visual impact. The basic rule is to use colours which give a good contrast such as black and red, black and green, blue and red. Avoid red and orange or red and green. Note that colour-blind people may experience problems distinguishing between some colours such as red and green.
6. Use darker colours for greater impact – red, blue, green and violet work well for text passages.
7. Use lighter colours for highlighting – orange and pink are especially effective, but where possible use a special highlighter pen.

If you want to write short crib notes on a transparency – to remind you about some facts, for instance – use a fine-tipped yellow marker. It won't be seen from the audience.

8. Use coloured ink to replace underlining it is more effective and distinct.
9. Most film manufacturers produce colour tinted transparencies that can make your presentation look effective, professional and above all more restful to watch than a glaringly white screen, especially in long presentations. You can get these coloured transparencies in yellows, and lighter reds, blues and greens.

    You can use marker pens on these tinted sheets but avoid colour clashes such as blue on a green background. Many tinted films are provided with a backing sheet so that they can be used in a plain paper copier, in which case black text can be copied on to the transparency.

Use different tints to separate out different sections of your text. If, for instance, you are dealing with the performance of your company you could use a different coloured transparency to deal with the UK, European and world markets or a different tint for each year's results and so on.

10. Most of the major suppliers produce coloured film that comes ready supplied with a bold coloured border surrounding a softer-tinted area. These are particularly good for titles or for presenting a particular section of the presentation.

The road ahead may not be easy ...

... the end result will make it worthwhile for all of us

11. When presenting graphics such as pie charts, histograms or graphs, it can be very effective to colour in whole areas for emphasis. This can be done in one of two ways:

   - use a broad tipped coloured marker;

   - use self-adhesive coloured film made specially for this purpose.

On your OHPs do not simply repeat what you are going to say: this makes it a "verbal" aid not a "visual" aid. Express your ideas pictorially and graphically.

12. Use colours that work well together. To be effective, your colour choice should emphasise the main text or graphic, provide a restful background and allow for effective highlighting. Here are some colour combinations that work well.

TABLE 2.3 Non-permanent OHP markers

Background	Text/graphic	Highlight
Blue	White, yellow	Magenta, black
Light blue	White, black, yellow	Yellow, white, black
Grey	Magenta, dark blue, yellow	Yellow, blue, crimson, green
Green	White, black	Crimson, white, black
White	Black, magenta, dark blue	Yellow, blue, crimson, green

Creating colour OHP transparencies as good as 35mm slides

This is quite easy to do. Suppose you want to use a colour photograph which shows off your products and uses the company logo in all its glory. Or you want to project a stunning colour visual which the graphics people have come up with to show your company accounts to good effect. The OHP is all you need. This is how to do it.

1. Prepare your original by laying out the photographs, artwork, etc. on a white backing sheet.
2. Once you are satisfied with your master copy, take it to a high street colour copy shop. They will feed it into their big colour copier and produce a transparency that will look as good as any slide. The price is around £2 per copy.

For even more spectacular effects on the OHP, send your originals to a litho printer who can make hundreds of copies on transparencies (very good if you want to circulate your OHP to sales people in the field).

Making your own illustrations

It is relatively easy to produce your own cartoons or graphics to help liven up your transparencies.

You can buy or borrow books of clip art where copyright has been waived.

1. Make a photocopy of the illustration/graphic you want to copy.
2. Use the enlarge or reduce facility to get the drawing to the right size to fit on the transparency.
3. Either:
   - trace the drawing on to the transparency by placing the original underneath the film, then simply draw round the illustration with a fine pen;

   or:
   - photocopy the image directly on to the transparency, making sure that you are using the appropriate film.

You can also copy clip art illustrations from specially designed software simply print out the clip art you want and photocopy it on to film or print it directly using your inkjet, laser or dot matrix printer.

"The bulb on the overhead projector once blew. The way I handled it was to call a tea break while the bulb was fixed which worked very well."

Catherine de Salvo, Fenman Training

Why use visuals?

- A picture is much more powerful than words.
- Visual images can portray meanings and ideas that words cannot.
- They save time – their message is much more quickly absorbed.
- They stay in the memory.
- They make your transparency much more interesting to look at.

"Words are not visuals … Discipline yourself to ask 'What will this slide show?' and never 'What will this slide say?'"

Anthony Jay, Effective Presentation

For OHP presentations to people up to 10 metres away, keep your typeface at a minimum of 18 points (5mm). 28 points (8mm) is better for most uses.

Always think, "Is there a visual way in which I can present this information?"

"Many business presentations start with an OHP transparency giving the presenter's name and position stating who you are. Because it is a traditional opening it tends to be dull. If you can make an original opening you will have a better chance of capturing your audience's imagination and attention."

Cristina Stuart, SpeakEasy Training.

Don't leave a visual up on the screen for too long – the audience may feel that there is some hidden message in it.

Try to avoid the use of too many abstract words or figures – use visuals instead. Figures 2.8 and 2.9 illustrate the difference.

	$bn
Imports:	
Goods	12.0
Services	8.4
Total	20.4
Exports:	
Goods	13.0
Services	6.3
Total	19.3
Balance of payments	(1.1)

Figure 2.8 Figures in a table
Figures presented in a table are difficult for many people to take in clearly, particularly if they are not familiar with seeing information like this on a day to day basis.

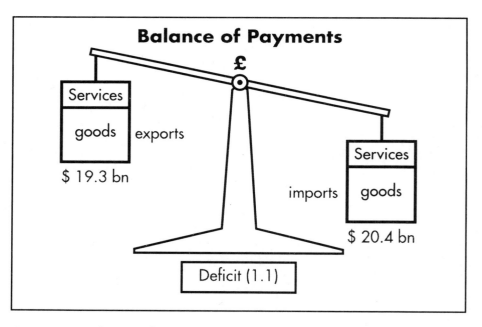

Figure 2.9 Showing figures with a graphic
If the figures are presented graphically it becomes easier to see the relationship between the figures. Your audience will be able to understand them much more easily and interpret the message you want to put across more accurately.

WHAT IS THE BEST WAY TO PRESENT NUMBERS?

Where possible avoid using a table full of figures. It is not only very dull to watch but there is a chance that the figures will not be seen. If you must present data, consider how you can get it across in an attractive and easily absorbed way. There are several different kinds of chart which could offer a solution.

Line graphs

Use line graphs for showing time series data, trends or information which consists of a large number of points of data (see Figure 2.10). If using colour, say for each line graph, do not overdo it. Keep the number of base colours to a maximum of five.

Five years ago we were only a small player in the market ...

... with our predicted growth over the next few years.

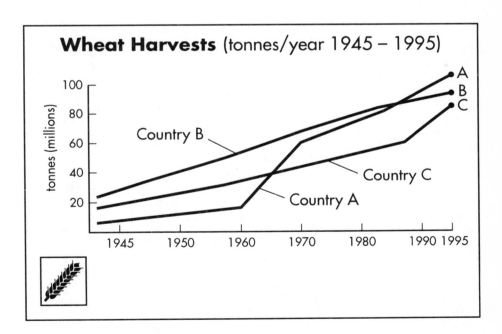

Figure 2.10 A line graph
A line graph is good if you want to show how a position has changed over a period of time and far easier for your audience to take in than putting up a series of numbers on a board.

Bar charts

Use bar charts when there is less data but you want to show comparisons between figures. (See Figure 2.11.) Bar charts can be made more sophisticated by giving them a 3D look and by careful use of colour. You can purchase special graphics and presentation software to construct charts.

> Always avoid putting too much information into one chart. Leave out as much as you can. Think about your audience. How quickly will they be able to take in the information?

Consider which kind of chart leads to the simpler presentation. Look at Figures 2.10 and 2.11. These charts show the same information – which is easier to read?

Graphs can handle more complex information much more simply and successfully from the viewer's point of view.

If a very complex chart is unavoidable, consider using a series of charts, rather than one, or an overlay technique (see below).

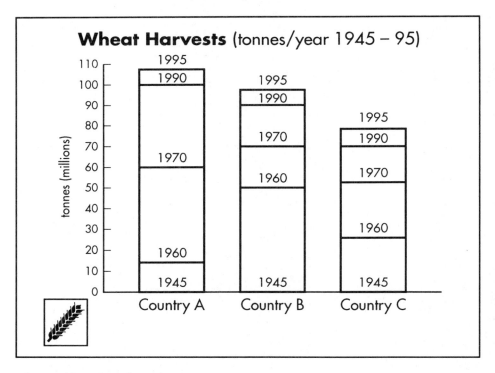

Figure 2.11 A bar chart
If you want to compare figures (e.g. the performance of a company from year to year or different divisions within a year) then a bar chart will be easier to comprehend than both a table of figures and a line graph (especially if there are a number of lines close together).

Flow charts

Flow charts are very useful for illustrating how things work, how parts fit together, or how a process operates. But there is a danger of showing too much in one chart. It can easily become a maze of boxes, arrows and lines which the viewer may take 10 minutes or more to absorb.

- Keep the flow chart easy to read and uncluttered.
- Break down the stages into simple units, showing no more than three or four boxes at any one time.
- Use colour to highlight different parts of the flow chart at different times.
- Reveal the chart gradually, rather than all at once.
- Build up a complex flow chart by use of overlays (see Figure 2.15).
- Take the audience through the flow chart carefully and check that they have understood.

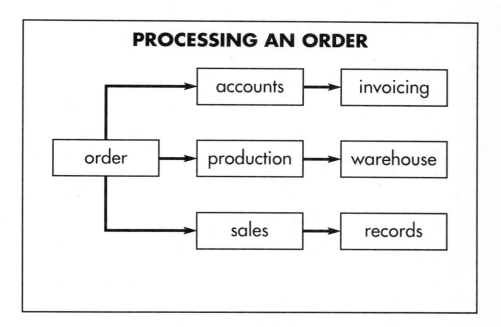

Figure 2.12 Using a flow chart to demonstrate how processes work
Flow charts are a good way of showing how different processes fit together. If you have a complex process to explain, break it down into mangeable chunks and build up the links step by step. The secret of good presentation with flow charts is not to feed too much information to your audience at once. Make sure they have understood what happens at each stage, before going on to the next.

Never express figures as a table. Put them into a bar chart or pie chart. Shown graphically they are far easier to comprehend.

Pie charts

Use pie charts to show how individual parts make up a whole (see Figure 2.13).

Pie charts can be made to look more interesting if each segment is drawn in a different colour, if the important segment/s are "exploded", or if a pie slice is broken down to a column of data to show how the totals were arrived at.

Always write the words in a pie chart horizontally – never let the angle of the "slice" dictate the word position.

Creating your own pie charts

There are four ways:

1. Use a ready-made pie chart tracing sheet such as the one produced by Schwan Stabilo.
2. Use a pie chart stencil. The stencil helps you to produce two- and three-dimensional pie charts.
3. Draw your own – you will need a protractor and a ruler.
4. Use spreadsheet or presentations software.

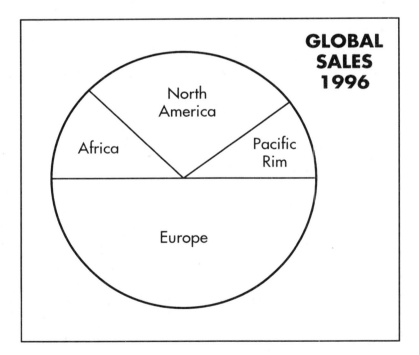

Figure 2.13a Pie charts

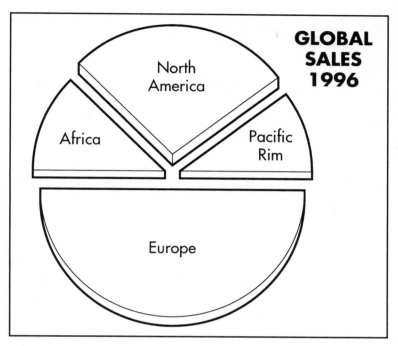

Figure 2.13b Pie charts
*Pie charts are a good way of presenting numerical information graphically.
Everyone is familiar with the slice of cake image. For comparisons (especially if
there are significant differences between the "slices") it is a quick way to grasp
the relationship between one slice and another. However, if your number of
slices exceeds four or five, present the information as a bar chart. Don't restrict
pie charts to numbers only. It is a good way of illustrating any information
comprising several parts that make up a whole.*

Suppose that you want to show how a total figure is made up of individual units:

* Divide an individual unit by the total sum.

* Multiply that figure by 360.

* This gives the angle in degrees of the wedge representing that unit.

For example, take the following output from a factory last year:

Units	Output	Unit/total	× 360 (degrees)
Washers	50	50/200 = 0.25	90
Bolts	75	75/200 = 0.375	135
Nuts	23	23/200 = 0.115	41
Screws	52	52/200 = 0.26	94
Total	**200**		

- Now draw a circle and from its centre draw a line to the 12 o'clock position.

- Measure an angle of 90° from that line and draw a line to the circumference. The resulting wedge shape represents washers.

- From the last line you drew, measure an angle of 135° to represent bolts; continue with screws and nuts.

 Water soluble marker pens used to create images on OHP transparencies can be wiped off simply with a damp cloth. To avoid accidental erasure use a permanent marker pen.

Using self-adhesive coloured film to make pie chart segments
You need the coloured film and a sharp scalpel or razor blade.
1. Draw a black and white master copy of the pie chart.
2. Make sure that the lines you draw are thick.
3. Photocopy this image on to a transparency.
4. Lay the coloured film over the transparency and, using a steel rule and scalpel, carefully cut out each pie segment using the middle of the thick line as your guide.
5. Tear off the backing sheet and loosely stick each pie segment to the underside of the transparency. Using the underside of the transparency allows you to write or draw over the surface without distorting the diagram.

 Make sure that there are no gaps between segments that are not covered by the thick black lines – this is to ensure that white light does not seep through the gaps.

  "I would recommend you use a border to your transparencies. It looks so much more professional. There are plastic sleeves available which have their own ready-made border into which you can slot your transparency."
Cristina Stuart, SpeakEasy Training

1 Outline area to be coloured on the transparency.

2 Cut a piece of colour film slightly larger than the area you intend to cover

3 Peel colour film from backing

4 Apply colour film to the reverse side of the transparency to cover the marked area.

5 Carefully cut colour film along the drawn contours using a knife.

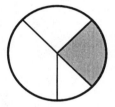

6 Remove superfluous colour film.

Figure 2.14 Using self-adhesive coloured film
If you want to add colour to your hand drawn pie chart segments use self-adhesive coloured film that can be cut out to the right shape and stuck to the back of your transparency.

ACCESSORIES FOR PRODUCING EVEN MORE PROFESSIONAL TRANSPARENCIES

Most of the main specialist suppliers produce a range of accessories that will help give transparencies an extra lift. Here are some examples.

Dry transfer lettering

You can produce a really impressive set of headings by using ready-made coloured characters. Nobo produces 5.5, 8 and 12mm letters in four colours. Schwan Stabilo produces rub-down lettering in three sizes of Helvetica semi-bold.

Transfer graphics

You can also use dry transfer graphics like the Nobo range with its circles, stars, arrows, lines, strips and assorted symbols showing people, vehicles, buildings and so on.

Made a mistake on an OHP transparency using a permanent marker pen? Don't panic, it can be erased using a spirit-based solution or a special correction pen designed for the purpose.

"A pack of wipes is very useful at an OHP presentation. The glass top is rarely cleaned well and it can spoil the appearance to have smudge marks in the middle of your transparencies."
David Martin, Buddenbrook Consultancy

Graphics guides

You can buy a whole range of draw-round guides and stencils that help you produce accurate and consistent lettering plus other graphics such as business symbols. There are even bar chart, pie chart and map of Europe templates available.

For a professional look, use a stencil guide and a grid-backed transparency to produce accurate lettering for your main points.

As with any OHP, if you use pre-produced graphics and lettering make sure that you concentrate on the centre of the transparency, avoiding the bottom third altogether. Remember to maintain adequate margins and to leave a good amount of space between the graphic and accompanying text. Don't squash things up!

"Don't forget your audience when using an OHP projector. There is a tendency for some people to talk down to the transparency. You must remember to maintain eye contact and to keep your head up. I like to move around the room and not stand rigid next to the projector as if it is attached to me."
Catherine de Salvo, Fenman Training

HOW DO I USE OVERLAYS?

One of the advantages of using transparencies is that images can be built up gradually by placing one sheet over another and so on. This is called the overlay technique.

Use overlays when you want to break down a complex idea step by step. This technique is especially useful for matters to do with:

* **geography** – maps and diagrams that build up;
* **biology** – building up a picture of a complex organism;
* **anatomy** – showing how parts of the body relate;
* **statistics** – building up complex data;
* **technical phases** – step by step build-up of a process by use of flow charts;
* **economic developments and cycles** – diagrams, graphs, data;
* **political themes** – inter-relating events.

These are just a few examples – it is possible to use overlays wherever you need to show the relationship between one transparency and the next.

The more transparencies you show at any one time, the less light will penetrate the film. Do not use more than five transparencies of normal film grade. Use less than five where the film is coloured or of a thicker grade.

Producing effective overlays

Use a Flip-frame or other mounting system to keep your transparencies exactly aligned. Do not use more than five transparencies, as with each one there will be a loss of transmitted light. Staedtler's Overhead Projection Handbook recommends the following procedure (see Figure 2.15).

1. Fix your first transparency to the frame's underside – this becomes the fixed base.
2. Add the first overlay to the top side of the frame, making sure that its image is fully aligned with that of the base transparency. Ensure that the first overlay can be opened outwards or upwards. This can usually be done by fixing the overlay to one side of the frame.
3. Fix the second overlay to the other side of the frame (opposite to overlay 1).
4. Fix the third overlay to the top of the frame.
5. Fix the fourth overlay to the bottom of the frame and so on.
6. Place the frame on the projector and simply turn each transparency on to the frame as you wish.

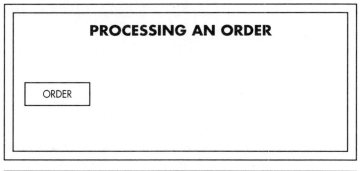

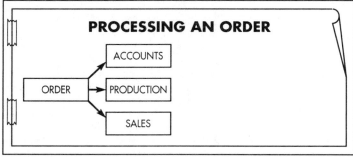

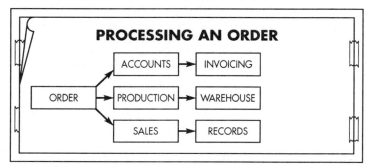

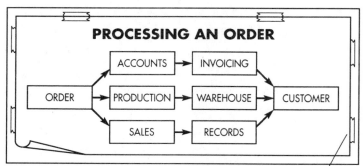

Use adhesive tape to fix each successive transparency to left, right and top of the frame.

Figure 2.15 The overlay technique

Overlays can be used to break down complex processes and show how the pattern builds up or how different parts relate to each other. For the overlay technique to be effective it is important that each transparency lines up accurately.   Source: Staedtler, Overhead Projection Handbook

Want to add a splash of colour to your black and white OHP transparency? Use special OHP highlighter pens which come in a range of bright fluorescent colours. To avoid smudging the image, use the highlighter on the reverse of the film.

Lining up the images on the overlays

It is very important that the image on each transparency is exactly in line with the film either under or on top of it. This is best achieved by using a special drawing board or by drawing each transparency in position in its frame. The simplest way to keep your overlays in line is to use a transparency pad – don't tear out any sheet until the image on each one is fully in line with the others.

Keep checking that your overlay is in line. You may want to use a fine-tipped yellow marker (water based) to provide a working outline before you commit yourself to a permanent image.

 "The way I tackle nerves is to use personal reassurances and say to myself that even if this goes really badly I am not going to die – I am still going to be able to go home at the end of the day and see my family."

Catherine de Salvo, Fenman Training

CREATING AN OHP PRESENTATION USING YOUR COMPUTER

Your computer can be used to create a master copy which can then be copied, using special film, onto a transparency. So anything you can do with your computer, you can get onto an OHP screen. This includes:

- writing text and transferring page layouts and blocks of text from your wordprocessing software;

- using a spreadsheet to present a list of figures;

- using graphics software to create artwork such as cartoons and illustrations;

- using special software to create the kind of graphics commonly used in presentations: charts, special lettering and so on;

- using a special device that projects whatever is on your computer screen up onto the OHP screen.

Using your wordprocessor

The wordprocessor is becoming more and more common in business functions. Most offices now have a PC (or AppleMac) on which text and data can be produced. Common packages, such as WordPerfect, Wordstar,

AmiPro, Word for Windows, Microsoft Works, mean that most people can create professional-looking documents. Some software will allow you to create text at a particular font size, design, put boxes around words, draw all kinds of graphics, and so on. Windows-based and Mac software is ideal for OHP presentations as it is based on a "what you see is what you get" (WYSIWYG) format. This means that the screen layout is exactly as you will see on the page and hence transparency. Before saving and printing your document, you can check what it is going to look like. (Windows and DOS are operating systems for IBM-compatible computers.)

There are difference in what looks good as a printed document and what is an effective OHP transparency. All the rules about word spacing, lines of text, size of text, using simple fonts and so on should be rigorously observed when you use your computer to generate transparencies.

1. Choose a wordprocessing or desktop publishing package that allows you to see what your document will look like before you print it out.
2. Choose a clear, simple font and a good size (for instance, Helvetica or Univers and a minimum font size of 18 point or 36 point for headings).
3. If appropriate, use the options in your software to draw boxes, circles, lines around your text.
4. Check the overall appearance of the page.
5. Save before printing.
6. Use the appropriate film for your printer.

The risks are great ...   Time is not on our side ...

Using special presentation software

There are several brands of specialist presentation software on the market. Essentially these are text and graphics packages which have been designed with the presenter in mind. They let you prepare attractive presentations quickly and easily – you don't have to be a design expert to produce some really effective transparencies or slides. The packages are designed for the busy business person who has little time to get to grips with complex software. They also often have "ready-made" templates that have already done much of the design work for you.

Templates allow you to produce a transparency or slide fast. They provide you with ready-designed layouts. All you have to do is add text, clip art or data into on-screen boxes. The presentation software has a range of charts and diagrams ready to use – you just supply your own data. In this way, colourful pie charts (two- or three-dimensional), bar charts, line graphs, flow charts, etc. can be created at the press of a button.

You can usually import text into presentation software from your normal wordprocessor or you can type directly onto the template.

Import artwork such as the company logo onto each page so that it is shown each time you project a transparency.

Presentation software allows you a choice of fonts, styles and artwork. You also usually get a freehand drawing tool to create your own artwork.

Presentation software currently on the market usually costs between £200 and £400.

TABLE 2.4 Presentation software

For Windows	Supplier tel. no.
Lotus Freelance Graphics	01784 455445
Aldus Persuasion	0131 453 2211
Microsoft Powerpoint	01734 270000
For DOS	
WordPerfect Presentations*	01932 850505

*Although DOS based, this uses a Windows-like environment.

Graphics

Many software packages provide graphic images that are either pre-drawn or are easy to adapt. You could also use software such as CoralDraw, Quattro Pro, MacDraw, DesignWorks or a desktop publishing package (Aldus Pagemaker, Ventura, Timeworks and so on) – they all have graphics capabilities.

Projecting images from your computer onto the OHP screen

New technology allows for exciting possibilities. Anything that can be shown on your computer screen can now be projected directly onto a screen without using a transparency! This means that you can prepare a computer presentation including text, graphics, even sound and animation using the latest CD-ROM technology. This presentation can then be shown in whatever order you command the computer to display each element.

To project computer images directly onto a screen you will need:

- a special LCD (liquid crystal display) projector that sits on the light desk of the overhead projector. This is connected to your computer (perhaps most conveniently a laptop) from which images are directed via the projector to the large screen;

- an OHP which is at least 400W in power. You cannot use a data display panel on a portable machine.

Motivate your audience to listen: use a rhetorical question to grab their attention. For example, "When most people have enough money to live, what can we do to motivate them to work harder?"

LCD projection panels are small boxes which sit on the OHP glass desk. They are produced by such companies as 3M, In Focus Systems and Polaroid. You can buy them in various stages of sophistication depending on whether you need to project in colour, or have moving images sourced from a video, CD-ROM or animation software. At the bottom end of the market are "static matrix" models which project only black and white text. The manufacturers usually produce their own presentation software to complement the system but anything that your computer shows can be projected onto an OHP screen. The more expensive models can present moving images, manipulate graphics, freeze the frame, insert blank screens, carry out automatic reveals, and so on.

Using an LCD projection panel

- See which colour combinations look good by testing the templates that come with the software package. Experiment with the panel's contrast and colour settings.

- Test the lighting conditions in the room where the presentation is to take place. Given that you are using a projector of at least 400W power you should not have to darken the room, but avoid placing the screen in direct sunlight.

- Set up the computer, panel, projector and screen well before the presentation is to begin. Test all functions and make sure that there is a backup bulb in the OHP.

- Prepare handout copies or other support material to give to participants.

"It can be quite useful to use a 'trigger' to get people to participate actively. Show them a video clip and invite people to comment on what they have seen or to compare it with their own experiences."

Catherine de Salvo, Fenman Training

Using a projection panel to create a slide show

Most presentation software, such as Lotus Freelance Presentations and WordPerfect Presentations, will allow you to create slides which appear in a pre-selected sequence. You can build up the slide to add text or graphics to the base image. For instance:

* Begin with a blank background.

* Add a background image (perhaps mountain peaks to suggest growth).

* Add text as a series of short bullet points.

* Fade one slide into the next.

* Add animated graphics such as a pie chart which gradually builds up or a bar chart which is drawn stage by stage.

The software allows you to choose the order in which the slides are to be shown.

All this can be programmed in advance so that one key stroke sets the presentation in motion (most projection panels will allow you to freeze frame or go back). You can have a remote control unit which also allows you to operate the projection panel from a distance

You must be alert to unauthorised personnel ...

We have been studying our competitors closely ...

Don't use more than four colours on any one transparency. The effect will be garish if too many colours are used.

HOW SHOULD I LOOK AFTER MY TRANSPARENCIES?

Although some of the acetates you produce you may only want to use once and then throw away, there may be others that you want to keep for repeated use. In either case, it is a good idea to treat the transparencies with a little respect: they can easily stick together and can be a nuisance to unravel during a busy presentation.

Here are some useful storage and retrieval tips that are worth a try.

The simplest and cheapest solution

- Store each transparency with its own backing sheet in a cardboard folder.

- Number each transparency by using a light yellow marker which will not be seen by the audience.

Transparent sleeves, mounts and other storage ideas

Most of the main presentation materials suppliers produce a range of storage and retrieval systems. These are all designed to keep the transparencies stable, tight and flat.

Transparent sleeves

3M and other producers make transparent sleeves or wallets surrounded by a frame into which punched holes have been placed to allow for storage in ring binder files. The 3M Flip-Frame™ has white opaque margins which can be folded back. These are ideal for writing notes which will not be seen by the audience.

Some manufacturers, such as Staedtler, produce a projection sleeve that contains the transparency. The sleeve itself can be placed on the projector without having to take the transparency out.

Don't forget to number your OHP transparencies in order of appearance. If they get out of order it will be easier to put them straight.

Card mounts

Card mounts are cardboard working frames which contain the transparency in a fairly permanent way (rather like the mounting for a 35mm slide). The sturdy frames make handling and filing easier, especially when they have punched holes for ease of storage in a ring binder or specially designed folder. You can often write or draw on the margin of these mounts, which is especially useful for numbering or making crib notes.

Filing transparencies

"I always keep my transparencies in a card mount stored in a record case. Each sheet is fixed to the card by masking tape. These mounts are much easier to handle and when you're in a hurry, there is less chance of fumbling and dropping the sheets. It also looks much more professional – having a transparency properly mounted and filed gives the right impression."

Sales manager of a cosmetics firm

Avoiding curling

Some grades of film tend to curl in the heat – this can be a nuisance if you want to use the transparency again. To avoid this problem you could:

- mount them in a card frame or Flip-Frame™ this is much the best way of using and storing transparencies;

- lay a piece of perspex or heavy duty OHP film on top during presentation.

If you are not using card frames or wallets, keep the each sheet backed with heavy copy paper or thin card. Do not rely on the tissue-thin backing paper usually supplied. It sticks to the film and tends to float away on the breeze of the projector fan.

TAKING CARE OF THE PROJECTOR

Projectors are fairly sturdy machines but they can be damaged if you:

✗ drop them;
✗ block the air intake, thus obscuring the cooling fan;
✗ leave the hinged overhead lens closed when the machine is switched on – this builds up damaging heat;
✗ leave them in full sun, where the powerful lenses could act like a magnifying glass and start a fire;
✗ cover them in chalk dust.

We have a
contingency plan ...

Savings have been
made ...

HOW DO I PREPARE THE ROOM FOR AN OHP PRESENTATION?

 "Most presentations take place in the wrong rooms. The room may have been built for one purpose, is being used every day for a second and is now adapted for a third your presentation."
David Bernstein, Put it together – put it across

Unless you are lucky enough to work in purpose-built presentation facilities, it is likely that the room in which you present will not be ideal for your talk. Wherever possible, try to see the room beforehand so that you can start to have a feel for it.

Minimum room requirements

Make sure that everyone in the room is comfortable and can:

- see you;

- hear you;

- be seen by you.

Setting up the room for your OHP presentation is an essential feature of a successful session. There are three essential elements to room design:

- seat layout;

- screen position;

- projector position.

 Avoid muddling the OHP transparencies up during your presentation by stacking them on the right hand side of the projector and after they have been displayed, put them down on the left hand side.

Seat layout

Assuming that you have the freedom to organise the seating plan to best effect, what kind of layout should you choose? The answer depends on the type of presentation. Here are some rough and ready rules you may find helpful, suggested by David Bernstein in *Put it together – put it across.*

Circle presentation (see Figure 2.16)
✓ Good for small groups.
✓ Use only in small rooms.
✓ Informal and comfortable.
✓ Excellent for interactive sessions.
✗ Not well suited to using visual aids as the audience is too near, and some may have their backs to the screen.

Horseshoe presentation (see Figure 2.17)
✓ You are in a central position.
✓ Discussion encouraged as people are face-to-face but can turn towards you.
✓ No one feels too far away.
✗ The angle of vision may not be suitable for some people.

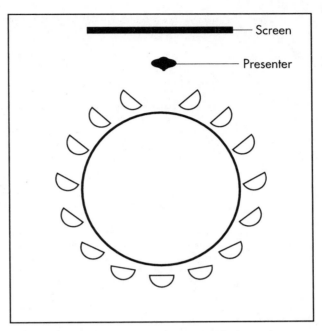

Don't forget to maintain eye contact with those closest
to you. It can be easy to overlook them.

Figure 2.16 Circle presentation
*This is good for small groups in an informal presentation keeping the group well
focused on the presenter but people may be too close for the presenter to use
visual aids effectively and some of them may have their backs to a screen.*

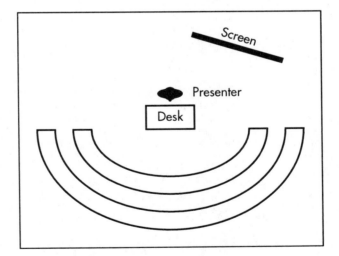

Fig. 2.17 Horseshoe presentation
*This is a good format for keeping the presenter in a central position and
encouraging the audience to interact with the presenter and with each other.
Some people may not be able to see the visual aids so you need to consider
carefully how your screen or chart is positioned to ensure everyone can see it
effectively.*

Give an audience longer to look at each transparency than you yourself need. Don't forget that you are familiar with the transparencies. As a rule of thumb allow your audience half as long again as it takes you to read the transparency.

Shallow V presentation (see Figure 2.18)

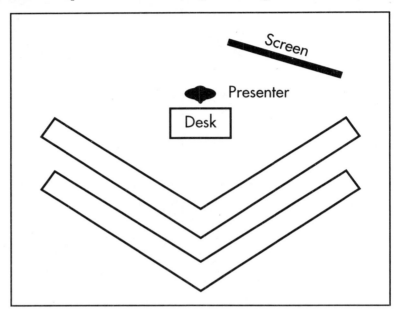

Figure 2.18 Shallow V presentation
This method may be better than the horseshoe format for everyone to see the visual aids.

✓ The same advantages as the horseshoe but more focused on you and the wall behind you.

✗ Its informality may not suit the presentation.

✗ You may feel "hemmed in".

Cafeteria layout (see Figure 2.19)

✓ Good for small group discussion stimulated by the presentation.

✗ Unsuitable for large groups.

✗ Less easy to keep the group focused on you and not on each other.

✗ The screen may be difficult to see for some people.

Theatre-style seating (see Figure 2.20)

✓ Particularly good for large groups.

✓ Allows space behind you where the screen can be seen by everyone.

✓ Provides a formal setting for the presentation.

✗ Not so good for discussion.

✗ People at the back may not be able to see above the heads of those in the front.

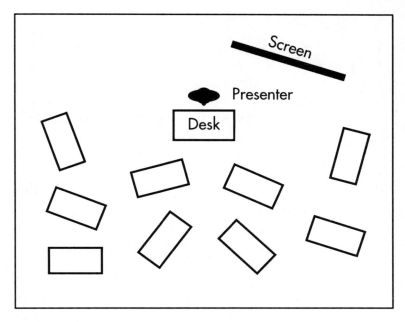

Figure 2.19 Cafeteria layout
The cafeteria method is good for small group discussion although some people may not be able to see the screen clearly. It offers a less formal and structured approach than the other formats.

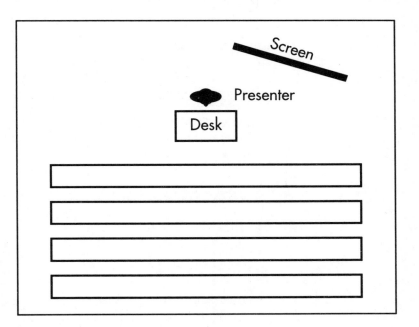

Figure 2.20 Theatre layout
A theatre layout is ideal for formal presentations involving large groups. For maximum visibility the audience should sit on raked seating. This format, however, is not ideal in situations where you want a good deal of interaction between members of the audience.

In a theatre-style layout, try to stagger the chairs so that the audience's vision is not obscured. Also make sure that the bottom of the screen is at least at eye level for those sitting at the back. In ideal circumstances you should either be raised on a platform or stage or the audience should be in raised raked seating.

Projector and screen position

Here are some simple rules to follow that will ensure that the image projected on the screen will be clearly seen by everyone in the room.

1. Place the projector as far away as possible from direct sunlight – a good place would be at the opposite end of the room to the windows.
2. Where possible, darken the area around the projector by dimming or turning off lights, by drawing blinds and so on.
3. At night make sure that there is enough room light for the audience to be able to take notes but not too much to dim the screen.
4. Position the projector between 1.8 and 2.5m from the screen – this will depend on the focal length of the projector lens (see Figure 2.21).

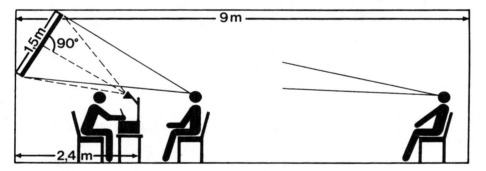

Figure 2.21 Positioning the angle of the projector
The projector needs to be between 1.8 and 2.5 metres from the screen. The lens part of the projector also needs to be positioned at 90° to the screen for an optimum clear image.

Source: Staedtler, Overhead Projection Handbook

5. Place the screen in a corner of the room if possible and as high as possible, so that even the bottom of the screen can be seen by the people at the back.
6. Make sure that the OHP screen doesn't obscure other visual aids you may wish to use (and vice versa).
7. Check for keystoning effects, where the image becomes a wedge shape rather than a rectangle – adjust the screen if necessary. Also look out for another common image distortion: fringe colouration, or red and blue tinges on the edge of the screen. Such colouration can be eliminated automatically by using an in-built lamp adjuster.

8. Remember the 1:6 rule about room and screen size – if the person sitting at the back is 30 feet away, the screen size should be at least one-sixth of that, i.e. 5 feet.square

If your OHP transparencies come with a backing sheet attached, separate the sheet from each transparency (but still keep a sheet between each one) before you give your presentation. This will make the process of showing each transparency much smoother and removes the danger of an embarrassing pause as you fumble to tear off a backing sheet which has become stuck to a transparency because of the static.

WHAT PREPARATION DO I NEED TO DO?

Before the presentation begins there are some things you should do to prepare and ensure that things go smoothly. Photocopy and use the checklist below each time you give an OHP presentation.

CHECKLIST – preparing to give an OHP presentation

The room:
- ☐ Is the chair layout to my liking?
- ☐ Can the room be darkened if necessary? If so, how?
- ☐ Are the projector and screen set up properly?

The equipment:
- ☐ Does the projector work?
- ☐ Does it have a working spare bulb?
- ☐ Am I familiar with its controls?
    - ✓ on and off switch;
    - ✓ focus knob;
    - ✓ image heightener;
    - ✓ bulb replacement switch;
    - ✓ light intensity control.
- ☐ Does the screen need to be assembled?
- ☐ If so, do I know how to do it?
- ☐ Is the screen high enough?
- ☐ Is the screen big enough?
- ☐ Is the distance between screen and projector correct?

Materials:
- ☐ Do I have all my transparencies?
- ☐ Are they in the right order?
- ☐ Can I handle the transparencies easily?

☐ Have I got all my supporting materials such as handout notes, crib sheets, and so on?

☐ Have I got a system for storing the transparencies once I have used them?

☐ Have I got enough pens?

☐ Do they all work?

☐ Have I got any spares just in case?

- Before starting the presentation, switch on the projector and use a trial transparency to test for correct focus and position. Make any necessary adjustments for keystoning, fringe colouration, screen positioning.
- Even if there is a back-up bulb in the machine, it makes sense to carry a spare lamp. Do not handle lamps when they are still hot and always carry them with a clean soft cloth.
- Rehearse taking the transparency on and off the projector glass. The smoother the changeover the more professional your presentation will look.

If your OHP transparencies do not have a backing sheet to them, insert an A4 sheet between each one. This helps to reduce the static that makes them stick together. It will also be much easier to read what is on each transparency.

"I use a coloured background for my transparencies. A yellow transparency which looks quite pale when projected is much easier on the eye than plain white. Alternatively, some people prefer to reverse out their lettering from a dark background."
Cristina Stuart, SpeakEasy Training

WHAT IS THE BEST WAY TO USE THE PROJECTOR?

1. Only keep the machine switched on if there is a transparency to be shown. If you are interrupted, you want to have a break or you want to make a point before showing the next transparency, switch off.

2. Switch the light on only once a transparency is in position; switch it off before you move the transparency away. This looks much more professional, it gives you time to line up your transparency and it avoids the full screen glare of an empty projector. There may be less need to do this if the transparencies move in very quick order (in which case consider using a film roll).

Switch off:
- as soon as you change subject;
- when you change a transparency.

3. When the projector is switched on, do not move the transparency around if you need to line things up, do this before you switch on.

4. Take care not to obscure the light source with your hand or shoulder.

5. If you are presenting sitting down, point where necessary to the transparency rather than the screen – use a pencil or pointer rather than relying on the shaky, magnified silhouette of your finger.

6. If you are standing, point to the screen again using a pencil or pointer.

When you use a pointer:

● Point at the screen, not at the transparency.

● Don't wave the pointer around but point to what you want to highlight and leave the pointer there until the audience has taken the material in.

● When you have finished pointing, put the stick down.

7. If you are writing on the acetate as you speak:
    ● sit down;
    ● rest your hand on the card mounting, margin or other edging material – avoid resting your hands on the film, you are likely to leave a large fingerprint;
    ● only use the upper two-thirds of the film;
    ● use an appropriate marker;
    ● have a cloth handy to erase any errors.

As a rule, try not to write on the transparency as you speak. It is very difficult to do well and it turns your attention away from the audience. Staring at the strong light is also uncomfortable. Use instead a flipchart or board.

Our competitors may be sailing along quite happily ...   ... we want to power ahead ahead of our competitors.

8. After using a marker, always replace the cap to avoid the ink drying out. Keep the pens away from the projector fan or desk, the heat can even dry out a capped pen!

9. Handling and storing the transparencies during the presentation:
   * Organise your work table so that on one side of the projector you have the transparencies in order ready to show. Number each where possible and check that the order is correct.
   * On the other side of the projector, pile up the used transparencies *in order* – this is important not only for future storage but because you may need to use one again in the question and answer stage.
   * At the end of the session store the transparencies away or throw them away – don't leave them discarded on the table, it gives a poor impression of the value you place on your material.

Animate your static OHP image with a cardboard cut out that can be moved over the transparency surface to create an animation effect to illustrate movement or changes.

"It is vital to give the audience enough time to read what is up there. I never read aloud what they can see – that's boring and rather patronising. Normally I allow one and a half to two times the length it takes me to read the transparency. I always check that everyone has finished reading before removing the transparency. If anyone is still having difficulty finishing reading, I am happy to let that person look at the actual transparency once I have moved on."
An experienced presenter in the confectionery business

SHOULD I USE THE REVEAL TECHNIQUE?

A reveal is a way of hiding part of the transparency currently being shown in order to present your information in stages or encourage the audience to think about the next step.

Should you use reveals in an OHP presentation? Many experienced presenters would say no. The reason is that covering part of your transparency may be distracting for the audience who keep wondering what it is you have to hide. Covering the projection table can also lead to a build-up of heat which could damage the machine.

✗ Where possible, avoid using the reveal technique in overhead projection. Instead use an overlay technique as described above.
✗ Avoid using the reveal technique with images – it is very easy to make it look wrong.

If you do wish to use a reveal technique with the OHP, cover up the part of the transparency you want to hide with some semi-transparent paper, such as ordinary white copy paper. In this way you can still see the information hidden but the audience cannot. Place the paper below the transparency to make sure that it is not blown away. (See Figure 2.22.)

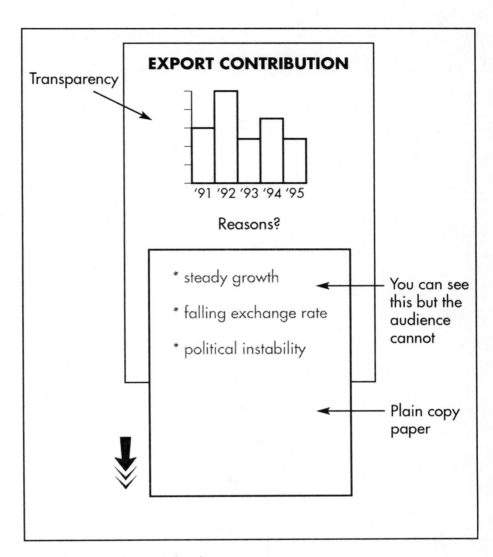

Figure 2.22 The reveal technique
If you reveal information in this way remember to keep the thin sheet of paper underneath the transparency. Otherwise the fan in the projector or other draughts can blow the sheet of paper away and steal your element of surprise by revealing the information to your audience before you intended to. Watch out as the sheet of paper gets closer to the edge of the transparency as it will be more difficult to keep the reveal in place.

A more systematic strategy for revealing part of the screen at a time is to place the transparency in a mount and use adhesive tape to stick flaps over the areas you want to cover and then expose (see Figure 2.23).

Need to write on an OHP transparency but worried about keeping the writing straight and legible? Use a lined backing sheet to the OHP to keep it straight and stencils for clear lettering.

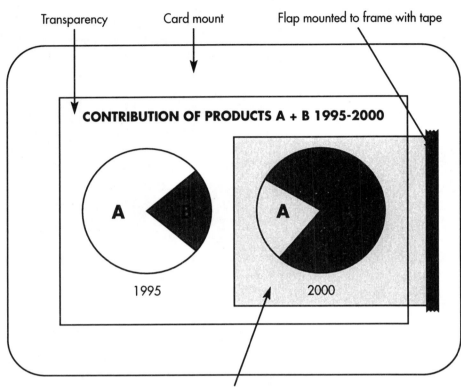

Transparency   Card mount   Flap mounted to frame with tape

CONTRIBUTION OF PRODUCTS A + B 1995-2000

A

B

1995

A

2000

Lift flap when ready to reveal pie chart 2000

Figure 2.23 Revealing your transparency step by step
*By taping over the relevant area of the transparency you can be more certain
that the sheet will not be blown away by any draught or fall off by accident.*

If you want to use a reveal technique think about using dark transparencies with
white lettering – this can be very effective.

CHECKLIST – using OHPs effectively

Before you go into your OHP presentation, check that you have made the
following preparations:

☐ I have checked that all the equipment I need will be in place and in full
   working order including:
   ✓ projector;
   ✓ transparencies in the correct order;
   ✓ pointer;
   ✓ pens to write on film (if required);
   ✓ OHP correction pen / erasure (if required);
   ✓ OHP wipes (if required).

☐ When preparing my transparencies I have used the correct film for writing on or using in my photocopier or printer.

☐ I have made sure my transparencies:
- ✓ are easy to read;
- ✓ are interesting to look at;
- ✓ use a mixture of text and graphics;
- ✓ use graphs and charts rather than tables of figures;
- ✓ incorporate some colour;
- ✓ follow the golden rules on lettering;
- ✓ are empty in the bottom third of the page;
- ✗ do not have blocks of typewritten text;
- ✗ do not have too many words per line or lines per page.

☐ I have stored my transparencies in a frame or mount and checked that all overlays are in order and ready to be shown.

☐ I have made sure that I can retrieve my transparencies quickly and easily.

☐ I have gone through the checklist on preparing to give an OHP presentation.

☐ I have rehearsed my presentation including introduction, main points and conclusion.

Not all OHP transparencies are suitable for putting through a photocopier. Transparencies made of acetate will melt with the heat of the copier. Those made of polyester can resist the high temperatures. Make sure your transparencies are suitable before you try to photocopy your masters.

Graphic ideas

The learning curve will be steep ...

We must strive for better quality ...

Flipcharts–

**be your own creative designer
and raise the applause**

3

"Illustrations can be used well on a flipchart. One speaker I witnessed giving a presentation about rockclimbing explained the system of ropes used and how rockclimbers are linked together for safety. She drew simply a side view of the rock face, two stick figures for the climbers and the ropes in different colours. Without that graphic, it would have been difficult to understand what she was explaining."

Cristina Stuart, SpeakEasy Training

WHAT KIND OF ROOM IS BEST?

Because flipcharts are not readily visible from a long distance, flipchart presentations are best given to small groups – under 10 is an ideal size. Use the rules below as a guide to ensure that the room is suitable for an effective presentation.

- It shouldn't be too big – people at the back should be no more than 3–4 metres away from the chart.
- It should be well lit – ideally any light source should be just in front of the easel.
- It should be well ventilated and heated.
- If an informal setting is required, there should be enough space for people to move around and come up to the chart to add their own points.
- There should be room on the walls to stick finished charts so that they remain visible.

If you can engineer when you are to speak, time it for first thing in the morning when people will be at their most alert. Avoid the spot immediately after lunch when audience attention spans shorten dramatically.

GET TO KNOW YOUR EQUIPMENT
The basics are:

* flipchart pad;

* easel;

* pens or markers;

* somewhere to store pre-drawn charts.

Let's look at some of the key points to remember about each of the basics.

 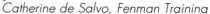

"The natural tendency with flipcharts is to write while you speak. That is not a good idea. If you are busy thinking about what you are saying rather than what you are writing it is easy to misspell words! Do one thing at a time."
Catherine de Salvo, Fenman Training

FLIPCHART PADS
A flipchart pad is essentially no more than a large notebook with tear-off pages. There are many brands around but most of the commercially available ones have the following points in common:

* They are either A1 size, 32" × 23" (813mm 584mm), or B1, 23" × 19" (584mm × 483mm).

* Each page is drilled at specific points to allow it to be mounted on the easel.

* They use high quality cartridge paper specially designed to prevent inks from bleeding through to the back of the sheet. Different weights of paper are available – at the top end are papers that resemble card which have a long storage life because they are much more durable. These heavy papers are expensive, however, and are not very portable.

* Some pads, like the Nobo A1 Squared pad, are provided with feint ruled squares to help keep lettering straight or for use as a chart plotter.

* Many products, such as those from Schwan Stabilo, are environmentally friendly – made from recycled paper using non-chlorine bleaches.

* The paper is perforated for easy tearing.

Want to keep your audience's attention focused on a particular part of the flipchart? Create a mobile pointer by cutting out a cardboard arrow and attaching Blu-tack to the back of it.

Types of pads to avoid

Some pads use newsprint paper which is thin, easily tearable and allows the inks to bleed through to the reverse side. Only contemplate using newsprint quality pads if your budget is very tight or if you don't mind using only one side of the sheet.

Special pads to look out for

- **Coloured pads** – your visual presentation can be simply yet effectively improved by using coloured pads. These can be purchased in pink, green, peach, lemon even black, but here you would need to use something like a fluorescent dry marker that can be easily seen.

- **Ready stuck pads** – these can be easily stuck to the wall as the presentation proceeds. Some, such as the Nobo Stick-it pad, become adhesive only when the sheet is smoothed, creating a static charge.

- **Re-usable pads** – these are made from a laminate which can be wiped clean. They are especially useful if you will want to make amendments during an interactive session.

Want to show a series of pre-drawn flipcharts and be able to locate each one easily? Create a series of tabs by folding a Post-it note over the edge of each chart and then number each note.

We are building the blocks for our future ...

Our competitor's share of the market is shrinking ...

   "It is a mistake to speak and write on a flipchart at the same time. Your audience's attention will be focused on what is being written so they won't be listening to what is being said."
Cristina Stuart, SpeakEasy Training

HOW DO I DESIGN AN EFFECTIVE FLIPCHART SHEET?

The key to any flipchart sheet can be summed up in one word: simplicity.

Remember that the main aim of the sheet is to summarise the key points you want people to remember about the presentation. There is a limit to how much information a person can take in at one time. For these reasons, it is essential that a flipchart sheet is clear, direct and relatively simple to grasp.

Flipcharts are essentially text orientated

Unlike other media, the simple flipchart lends itself well to a text-based presentation. But whereas significant detail can be given in the form of a handout or other printed notes, the flipchart is easily over-filled. In order to have impact it is important not to have too much text on each page.

Use abbreviations liberally especially on longer words. A simple trick is to leave out the vowels or chop off the end of a word – it is still easily understandable :
    Mgt – Management;
    Mngr – Manager;
    Co – Company;
    Dept – Department.

Here are some useful tips for presenting text.

- Emphasise key points by putting words in a box.

- Write out the word first and then draw the box around it.

- It looks better if you keep all boxes the same width but extend the depth to encompass more words. (See Figure 3.1.)

- Use squared paper to help you keep lines of text straight and to keep margins, bullet points or subheadings in line.

- If 'during the presentation' you want to add text to a complicated graphic (say a series of boxes or a flow chart), try drawing the outline in faint pencil before the session begins, or draw the outline in thick marker pen on a sheet placed behind the one you will be using to write on.

Be visible!
One of the most important features of using the flipchart is that the text you write must be easily and comfortably visible to every member of the group. Text should be interesting and pleasant to look at.

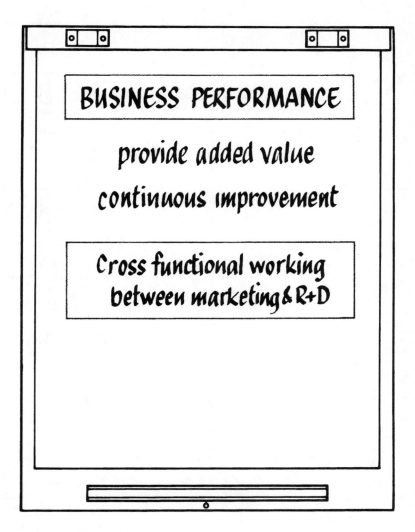

Figure 3.1 Emphasise key points by using boxes to highlight
Boxing key words is an effective way of highlighting points. For a professional finish keep all the boxes the same width. Extend the box vertically instead if you want to fit in more text.

Some useful rules of thumb for text:

1. Have no more than 6–8 lines of text on each sheet. Figure 3.2 looks much better than Figure 3.3.

2. Make sure that people at the back of the room can read your smallest text easily. Remember that the person you are trying hardest to impress may be short-sighted and sitting at the back of the room!

3. Keep the text size large enough. Ideally your writing should be around 15–20mm (up to ³/₄") in height.

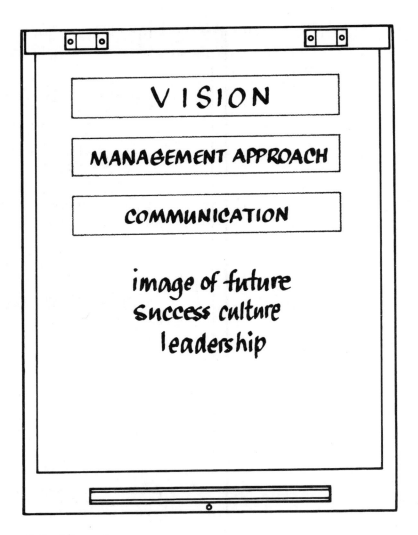

Figure 3.2 6 lines ✓
Six lines to a flipchart is much clearer than twelve. It will help you to keep your text to a good size. Remember, the fewer the words the bigger the impact.

Do you have trouble writing clearly at the bottom of a flipchart pad? Simply pull the bottom of the flipchart up to a more comfortable height.

"The success of an opening has a lot to do with how relevant it is to your audience. When I am giving a presentation to trainers I will ask them what they want to get out of the session, record those answers on the flipchart and refer back to them in the presentation. If people can see there is something in it for them they will sit up and listen."

Catherine de Salvo, Fenman Training

Figure 3.3 12 lines *X*
This looks too crowded. Your audience will not be able to take in the text very clearly and may leave the meeting with a confused message or (worse) the wrong one.

Our competitors will find it difficult to survive ...

The competition is crushing everyone ...

Keeping your flipchart clear and visible

- If you are right-handed, stand to the right of the chart with the audience on your left (and vice versa for left-handers). This means that you won't have to obscure the chart as you write on it.

- Use printed lettering in BLOCK CAPITALS for headings and lower case for other text avoid longhand. (See Figure 3.2.)

- Don't let the text slope downwards as it nears the right-hand edge of the sheet (see Figure 3.4).

Figure 3.4 Don't let the text slope down
If you stand too far to the left of the flipchart, you will find it difficult to keep the lines straight and your text may slope down. The best position (for right-handers) is to stand mid-way on the left-hand half of the flip-chart (and vice versa for left-handers). If you still find it difficult to keep your lines straight, flipchart pads with feint ruled squares are available.

* Try to be consistent in the way that you write the text. Don't keep changing the style of your writing – this will only distract your audience and the sheet won't look professional.

* Write as quickly as you can without affecting style and visibility. Slow and deliberate writing will disturb the viewer's concentration and you may lose that essential eye contact with your audience.

 "If you have to draw something on a flipchart 'spontaneously' draft an outline in light pencil first. This is useful for calculations and those speakers who suffer from poor spelling."
Cristina Stuart, SpeakEasy Training

Which colours should I use?

Most marker pen manufacturers offer a good range of primary colours at least. Colour will add interest and impact to your flipcharts. It can be used to great effect for emphasising certain words or discriminating between two points of view.

* **Red** is excellent for emphasising or underlining a word but do not use it as main text, it is difficult to read at a distance.
* **Black** and **blue** are ideal for main text. **Green** is next best in terms of visibility.
* The least visible colours are **purple**, **brown** and **pink**. The worst is yellow!

Mixing colours can add great interest to your chart but try to avoid using more than three in any one sheet.

Avoid colours which clash and are harsh on the eye:
* orange and blue;
* red and green;
* yellow and red.

How to use bullet points

Bullet points are symbols which emphasise different points and distinguish between them. They can be used as an alternative to numbering a list of points, which may be falsely interpreted as some order of priority. Bullet points are also considered to be more attractive than numbers.

Use a consistent bullet point design to separate out distinctive points. These bullets can be in the form of asterisks, ticks, stars, arrows or filled circles, triangles or squares:

* asterisks;
✓ ticks;
★ stars;
→ arrows;

● filled circles;
▲ triangles;
■ squares.

To reveal information using a flipchart – don't fold the sheet up, the writing often shows through from the back, making it look messy. Instead, cut out strips of paper to cover the key words you want to reveal and use Blu-tack or a non-permanent glueing system for paper such as Pelikan's Roll-fix which tacks paper down but can be peeled off as required.

Useful design techniques

You don't have to be a professional graphic designer to design any visual aid in a really effective way. What you need are a few general pointers on how to make a page of text (or graphics) look interesting and have maximum impact. There is nothing more dull to look at than a page of text filling up a flipchart sheet. However interesting the content of your presentation, you will want to keep the attention of the audience who will certainly spend much of the time looking at the flipchart. The ideas below are just a start.

1. **Use key words or phrases to summarise a point.** As an example here are some ideas elicited from a session on approaching a customer:

    * "Give them time to look around."
    * "I always keep in the background – give them space and they'll show you what they're interested in."
    * "Move closer only when you see them handling a product or if they're obviously looking for help."

    This could be written on a flipchart as:

If you are not familiar with writing on a flipchart try to get some practice to feel what works best for you. To increase legibility you may find it helpful to create your letters in two or three strokes. For example, a W can be created as two Vs; an R in three strokes. It will feel different from your handwriting where you are used to creating letters and words in one stroke but is worth the practice. Still aim to keep your writing flowing though.

2. **Use a simple graphic to replace a string of words.** It is often said that a picture is worth a thousand words. Research shows that of the information taken in by our senses, over 50% is visual, under 40% is what we hear and the rest is from the other senses.

   Visuals can be particularly useful because:
   - they create interest and impact;
   - they can represent quite complex ideas;
   - people tend to remember them.

   As examples you could use:
   - an oak tree to symbolise growth;
   - ! for "warning";
   - stick men for various actions;
   - simple faces to show emotions such as happy or sad (☺ or ☹);
   - an egg-timer to show the passing of time.

On flipcharts write your notes on the flipchart itself in a light pencil. Don't make the notes too small (the audience will not be able to read them because they are in pencil) and keep them at eye-level, not low down on the flipchart. Bending over to peer at tiny lettering will not impress an audience.

If you can't draw even the simplest of graphics, trace a pre-drawn one on the page behind the current sheet, or prepare a cut-out that you can draw around or simply stick on the chart with double-sided tape. Books of traceable/copyable graphics are available.

3. **Keep plenty of white space.** This helps to make the flipchart look more interesting. Leaving plenty of room for margins top, bottom, left and right will help to avoid a cluttered look. A simple rule of thumb is to leave a 4" margin around the sheet (the fewer words on the sheet, the bigger the margin). You may want to leave a bigger margin at the bottom than the top – this looks good and allows people at the back to read the whole page.

4. **Charts** can be very effective in the display of numerical information or, as in the case of pie charts, relative proportions of things to a whole – such as the proportion of total expenditure devoted to overheads and direct costs, or how an area of farm land is used, and so on.

Bar charts or histograms are useful to display trends over time by comparing two or more variables. (See Figure 3.5.)

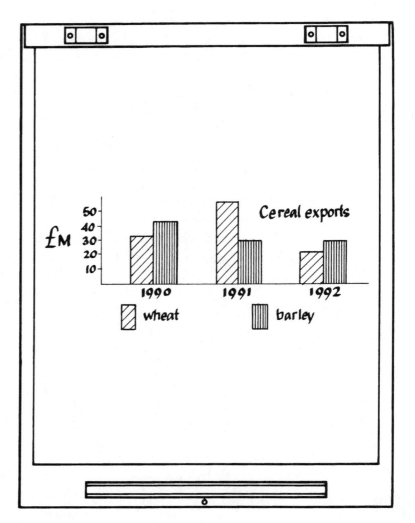

Figure 3.5 Bar charts can show two or more variables over time
Use bar charts to display numerical information. You can use them to compare the performance of different products between years. Use different colour markers to shade the boxes and highlight the difference between the bars. If you find you don't have a different colour marker to hand, shade the boxes with different angles to distinguish between the bars. Don't forget to provide a key for your audience of what the different shaded bars mean.

You can even produce three-dimensional bar charts which are visually very effective, especially where there are two or more variables on the horizontal axis. (See Figure 3.6.)

5. **Graphs** are used to show trends and the relationship between one variable and another. Use them especially where there are three or more variables to consider – graphs can be easier to read than bar charts.

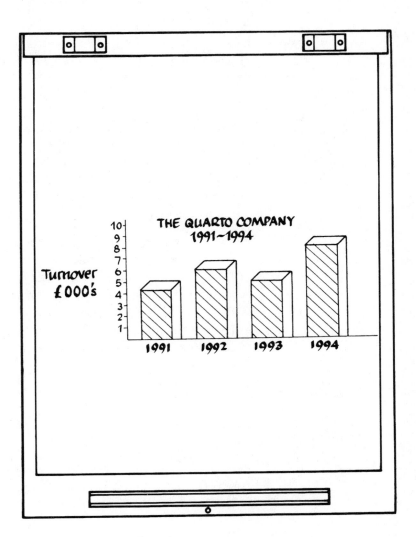

Figure 3.6 Drawing a 3D bar chart
To make your charts stand out, turn them into three-dimensional charts. To do this successfully it is better to leave a gap between one bar and the next. To draw the 3D effect accurately it is useful to plot the corner points first before joining up the lines.

Some people feel uncomfortable writing on a flipchart and keeping their back to the audience at the same time. Unless you are a contortionist it is very difficult to write and keep facing the audience. By all means turn your back on them to write, but remember to face the audience again once you have finished.

6. Flow charts are usually shown as a series of boxes and arrows. They are useful for illustrating a sequential process, such as how to print from a negative or how to apply for a loan. There should only be one or two words in each box and there should not be too much to read in any one chart.

   If you are taking people through a flow chart, do so at the most appropriate speed for your audience. If necessary reveal the boxes one by one. There is more on reveals in the next section.

It is a good idea to draw the flow chart in advance if possible. You could draw in the boxes and the arrows and leave any wording for the presentation.

7. Use tables of figures with extreme caution. It is all too easy for a chart to become an unreadable mass of rows and columns of figures. Here are some handy tips:

   * Help your audience to focus on the figures to be looked at by using colour or some kind of stick-on ring.
   * Draw column rules in pencil in advance so that you keep the figures straight. This also helps you to ensure that there is enough room on the sheet to include all your data.
   * Draw horizontal lines so that your figures stay in the correct row and column (this and the previous point could be avoided by using ready-ruled paper).

The golden rules with all charts are:

☐ Keep them simple!
☐ Don't make them too pretty.
☐ Make sure that all the figures and words can be read easily.
☐ Keep the information to be read to a minimum.
☐ Avoid writing text in any way other than horizontally.
☐ Make sure that the page looks good.

Remember the 3 Ps!

The secrets are good flipchart presentation:
● Position
● Preparation
● Practice

 "Don't worry about pauses while you are writing on the flipchart. I think silences are useful and what seems a long time to you won't seem like a long time to your audience. People won't be sitting there with blank minds – hopefully they will be sitting there thinking about points that can be included on the flipchart."
Catherine de Salvo, Fenman Training

... the rewards make
it worthwhile ...

We must not get knocked
off our course ...

HOW DO I USE THE REVEAL TECHNIQUE?

The reveal technique is a way of gradually uncovering pre-drawn or pre-written material during your presentation. Why use a reveal?

- It saves time in writing during the presentation.

- You can synchronise your speech and the flipchart information.

- It provides the audience with something interesting to watch.

- It allows you time to set out your material in a neater, perhaps more attractive way.

 Don't try to talk your audience and write on a flipchart at the same time. They may not be able to catch all your words if you talk away from them. Also, if they start to respond to what you are saying it will interrupt your flow and may cause you to make mistakes.

Method 1

Bring the bottom of the page up to cover the text at the top. Use masking tape to keep it in place: double the masking tape over on itself and place in the bottom corners of the sheet. (See Figure 3.7.)

✓ Easy to do.
✓ Allows you to move away from the chart.

✗ Page ends up with unsightly fold marks.
✗ Printing may show through (avoid using marker pens).

A variant of this method is to use a large piece of paper to cover the chart you are using and tape it in the same way.

Figure 3.7 Folding the flipchart up to create a reveal
The beauty of this method is its simplicity. Watch out that people cannot read the reveal from the underside – or by looking through the gap!

Method 2

Cover the points you want to conceal with strips of double thickness paper. Use double-sided tape but not more than 3mm at a time. Tape or glue the inside bottom corners of each strip to stop it curling.

✓ You can conceal parts of the chart and not necessarily from top to bottom perhaps the left-hand or lower right side.

✓ You can show the whole chart with some gaps to be filled in later by removing a strip. (See Figure 3.8.)

✗ If the concealed section is too wide or long, the strips may fall – off if a wide reveal is necessary (say more than 30cm) tape the centre of the strip as well.

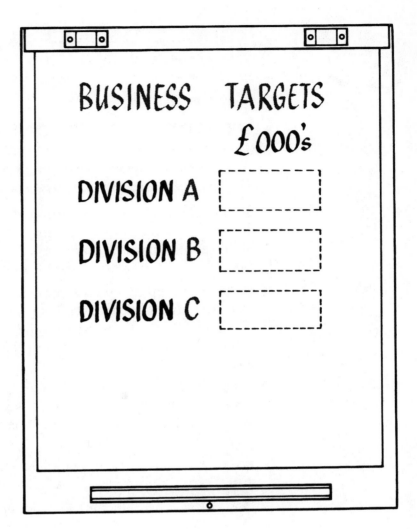

Figure 3.8 Concealing part of a flipchart with a reveal
Using a double thickness piece of paper to cover up information you want to reveal later is a neater way than folding the flipchart. You can be more selective about the information you cover up. Use a non-permanent glueing system such as Pelikan Roll-fix. Make sure the glue is applied to the edge of the reveal and is not directly on any letters in case it lifts part of it off. Try it out before you begin your presentation.

- Think through in advance how you are going to use the reveal technique.

- Don't cover up a title that is rather overdramatic.

- Think carefully about the timing of removing the paper over the concealed text or graphic. Remove just as you reach the point or just as you are about to leave it.

- Have some spare masking tape ready to repair any strips that may fall off.

 "Effective flipcharts should be in strong colours such as black or blue with other colours as highlights. Remember that red and green may be difficult to see from a distance and can be confused by someone who is colour blind."

Cristina Stuart, SpeakEasy Training

FLIPCHART PRESENTATIONS WITH A DIFFERENCE

Although a flipchart seems a simple and perhaps rather low-tech medium, with a little imagination you can turn your presentation into a really professional event. Consider these suggestions:

1. **Use two flipcharts.** One chart uses prepared sheets which help to introduce the concepts and ideas in a more formal way – perhaps professionally drawn. The other is blank and is used to elicit ideas from the group and summarise key points from any discussion.

2. **Combine the flipchart with another medium**, say a slide projector, video recorder or an overhead transparency. The flipchart can then be used for what it does best: conveying key points with words. The other medium can be used in conjuction with the flipchart, perhaps to show quite complex images.

3. **Use a pointer.** Cut out an arrow or other shape. Stick a piece of Blu-tack to the back of this and it can be used as a mobile pointer which can be placed anywhere on the chart. The same can be done with any symbol or shape that suits your message.

4. **Use an A3 photocopier to enlarge charts, drawings and photographs.** Stick or staple these to the sheet for an effective and professional look.

5. **Consider using a computer-based plotter to draw colourful graphs and charts.**

 For small amounts of text on a flipchart use capitals or print your letters. It will be easier to keep your writing consistent and legible. Never use script – it will appear too small and be difficult to read.

 If you mean to use charts again, make sure that not only are they properly stored but they are carefully numbered. You can mark in a sheet number or reference in yellow ink which will not be visible from the audience.

 "The secret of a good flipchart presentation is to invite the audience to make suggestions of what the key points are. By making them believe they are producing the flipchart you have captured their attention and give them the feeling of being really involved."

David Martin, Buddenbrook Consultancy

TROUBLESHOOTING

Prevent ink bleeding through to the page underneath by:
- stapling two pages together to prevent this;
- only using marker pens specially designed for flipchart use;
- using good quality cartridge paper.
- Marker pens do dry out – always have spare ones ready.

Want to spice up a flipchart or a transparency with a graphic but drawing is not your strong point? Select a simple image from a clip art book or other source, (enlarge or reduce it on a photocopy if necessary), trace the image onto a piece of card, cut out the outline you want to appear using a sharp scalpel and you have a ready to use stencil that can be used time and time again to produce professional images.

CHECKLIST – Preparing to give a flipchart presentation

You might find it useful to refer to this list every time you are going to give a flipchart presentation.

Position:
- ☐ Can the chart be seen by everyone?
- ☐ Can I stand with the chart to my right (and vice versa for left-handed presenters)?
- ☐ Is the chart firmly fixed?
- ☐ Is the room ready?
- ☐ Where can I Blu-tack or pin individual sheets if necessary?

Preparation:
- ☐ Is a flipchart the best form of presentation for the occasion?
  - ✓ It is quite a small group.
  - ✓ I want group discussion.
  - ✓ I want members of the group to add their own ideas.
- ☐ Have I got some spare markers?
- ☐ Have I prepared drawings or other complicated ideas in advance?
- ☐ Have I rehearsed (if possible)?
- ☐ Have I numbered the sheets to ensure they remain in the correct sequence?
- ☐ Have I tested all marker pens?
- ☐ Have I brought along different coloured marker pens?
- ☐ Have I prepared a script or crib notes?

Practice:

☐ Can I write neatly and make sure that my letters are large enough?

☐ Can I keep the number of words to a minimum?

☐ Do I know how to use illustrations and graphics where possible?

☐ Do I always talk to the audience, never to the chart?

☐ Do I use colour?

☐ Can I use reveals if necessary?

Need a memory jogger when writing on a flipchart? A light pencil or yellow marker will not be seen by your audience.

Whiteboards –

**add a dash of spice
to the white space**

4

 "Humour in presentations needs to be treated with great care. What makes people laugh is often not the content, it is the timing and delivery."

Cristina Stuart, SpeakEasy Training

GET TO KNOW YOUR EQUIPMENT

The humble whiteboard can be an extremely effective visual aid. Many presenters prefer the width of the whiteboard for active brainstorming sessions where ideas may be coming thick and fast. There are many shapes and sizes of board to fit any space – there are even ones that hang on rails that can be rolled around corners.

For a whiteboard presentation you need:

* the board;

* a good set of markers;

* an effective board eraser.

Pens and markers

It is essential that, when using a whiteboard, you use a pen or marker designed for the job. If you don't, you may find that the ink cannot be wiped away, or it may leave an unsightly ghost mark.

Important features to look out for when choosing a whiteboard pen:
* **A snap-fit cap** to prevent the ink from drying out.
* **Low odour** – for many people the pungent alcohol-based odour of the old-style whiteboard pens was an unacceptable irritant. Modern pens overcome this problem.
* **Pen-style clip** for easy storage.

- **A range of colours** – for example, Papermate, Stabilo and Nobo offer between them red, green, blue, black, brown, violet and orange. Packs or wallets of assorted or one-colour pens can usually be found in stationers.
- **A choice of line widths and nibs** – there is usually a choice of chisel nibs which give a bold thick line or a finer bullet-tip. Tips range from 4mm (for example the Nobo Jumbo, ideal for thick bold lines) to fine 1mm pens such as the Nobo Pencil.
  – Stabilo offers a bullet tip with a 2–3mm tip and a 2–6mm chisel nib.
  – Papermate's two markers are 3–4mm for the M34 and 1.6mm for the bullet-tipped F37.
- **Fluorescent colours** – some manufacturers offer bright, fluorescent markers which can help underline a special point on the board or pep up a diagram.

Before you start writing on a whiteboard ask yourself how much material will appear on it and plan your space at the start. Think ahead to the end of the line – don't cramp your letters in and abbreviate if necessary.

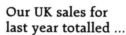

Our UK sales for last year totalled ...

Our strategy for next year ...

Nobo drymarkers are refillable.

Cleaning the whiteboard

The great advantage of the whiteboard is its pristine white surface which can be wiped clean for the next person to use. The problem is that if the board is not effectively cleaned it can lead to a ghosting effect, where the marks of previous presentations are still visible. This gives a very bad effect for any presentation.

It is a good idea to wipe your board thoroughly after use – text that stays on a board for two or three days becomes very difficult to remove completely, even if you have used a non-permanent marker.

Although a dry wiper can be used, and is often more convenient, you will get much better results from using a damp cloth or sponge – but make sure that there isn't too much moisture on the cloth or the board itself will become wet, making it very difficult to produce sharp text and diagrams.

You can use proprietary board cleaners such as Quartet's GhostDuster – a very effective impregnated pad which absorbs the dust. The same company also produces moistened towels which can be thrown away after use. In addition there are a host of sprays, cleaners and liquids on the market to help keep your whiteboard white.

Another problem is the build-up of grease and pigment particles even over a short time which tends to make the whiteboard look grimy. It is a good idea to give the board a regular clean with something like the Stabilo Whiteboard liquid cleaner, which comes in either a bottle or pump spray. Any alcohol-based cleaner can be used, or a little diluted bleach and water. Always make sure that you rinse the board and wipe it dry after any cleaning.

If you have used a permanent marker on the whiteboard by mistake permanent marker ink can always be removed by using special whiteboard cleaner (spit and even cigarette ash also seem to work well!).

"If you suddenly forget your words, the best advice is not to panic. Take a deep breath and pause. The immediate reaction is to plough on and muddle through. By doing this you end up saying something you have already said or stumbling over your words. Even if you say something like 'I have lost my track, let me just gather my words', your audience will accept that much better than if you try to carry on. Making a real mess of it just makes your audience feel uncomfortable. Stop, pause and collect your thoughts together."

Catherine de Salvo, Fenman Training

HOW CAN I KEEP MY WHITEBOARD INFORMATION?

Unlike flipcharts, whiteboard contents cannot easily be stored. If you do need to keep the information that has been written on the board, and it is not already available in handout form, consider taking a photograph of the whole thing. You could use an instant development camera or any conventional piece of equipment to record your whiteboard contents.

If your budget allows, you could consider electronic boards which incorporate a moving scanner that allows what you have written to be copied and printed onto A4-sized sheets. An example of this are the Nobo Electronic Copyboards which come in freestanding or wall-mounted versions.

Another option is to get a special board copier such as the Casio CP1000. This acts like a desktop camera which focuses on the whiteboard (or flipchart) images and produces a copy.

Don't worry about obscuring the whiteboard while you are writing. But remember to stand back for everyone to see the board as soon as you have finished writing.

PEPPING UP THE WHITEBOARD

Lettering

A whiteboard presentation can look really good if the lettering used is large enough and is straight.

One way to keep your text lines straight is to draw guidelines before the presentation. If this is done with, say, a Lumocolor Superfine 311 pen in yellow, it will hardly be noticed. Alternatively, you could use a board that has a ready-marked permanent grid.

Print letters but don't use capitals all the time. Vary the text by using upper and lower case. (See Figure 4.1.)

> This is much more pleasant to read than
> THIS SCREAMING HEADLINE TEXT—
> JUST IMAGINE A BOARD FULL OF THIS
> Imagine trying to read this script sitting
> at the back of the room — not easy is it?

Figure 4.1 Making the whiteboard easy to read
Use capitals for headings but vary your text by printing lower case letters for the main text. This makes it easier on the eyes of your audience than if it it is all capitals. But take care not to use longhand – this is even harder to read than capitals.

To help you write in a straight line without using pre-drawn rules move your writing hand along left to right by using all your arm and not just the wrist. A little practice here will go a long way.

There is no passport
to success ...

There are two
possibilities ...

Colour

Markers come in many bright colours and you can get fluorescent markers such as the Nobo Fluorescent Drymarker or the Staedtler Top-star range. Black, red, green and blue are the easiest colours to see. Use yellow and brown for shading or underlining. Use fluorescent colours to make things stand out (but do not overuse them).

Use two or more colours to distinguish between different sets of ideas.

Colour can also be used to highlight key points. You could use, for instance, different colours for alternate lines or to highlight a mnemonic.

Worried about your spelling? Use the remark which has been attributed to Mark Twain to get over any hiccups with your audience: "If you can only spell a word one way you are not being very creative. I just like to be creative".

HOW DO I PREPARE FOR A WHITEBOARD PRESENTATION?

The room

Whiteboards, like flipcharts, are only visible to a limited extent. They should not be used in large groups – 30 is the limit but around 10 people is ideal.

Be visible

As with a flipchart, it is essential that your letters or graphics are visible from the back of the room. Practise writing with block letters at least 15–20mm high. If the room is longer than 30 feet, use 30mm high lettering.

CHECKLIST for a whiteboard presentation

☐ The room is not too big – people at the back should be no more than 3–4 metres away from the board.

☐ The room is well lit – ideally any light source should be just in front of the board. Check that the light source doesn't reflect off the shiny board.

☐ The room is well ventilated and heated.

☐ If an informal setting is required, there is enough space for people to move around in and come easily up to the board to add their own points.

☐ I have a good range of suitable markers.

☐ I have an effective board eraser.

35mm slides –

put yourself in the limelight with bold, sharp images

 "The advantage of 35mm slides is that they are more professional. They are particularly impressive if you have two projectors so that you can diffuse one image into the next which avoids the 'clink clunk' as one slide changes sharply to the next."
Cristina Stuart, SpeakEasy Training

GET TO KNOW YOUR EQUIPMENT

The basic requirements for a slide presentation are:

- a collection of 35mm slides;
- a slide projector;
- a screen.

 What is the very first thing you should do in front of your audience? Smile and maintain eye-contact with them. This will break down the barrier between you and make them think "he looks friendly". If you frown or have a worried look on your brow, your audience will only think "he looks nervous".

PROJECTORS

The key features to look for in a projector are:

- a remote control function – very important as you may want to be closer to the audience or screen than the projector;
- a remote control unit which allows you to adjust focusing;
- a carousel-type loading system (or magazine) so that the slides can be placed in position before the presentation begins.

The rotary carousel system takes more slides than the conventional magazine – the rotary carousel can take up to 170 slides depending on the thickness of the slide. To be effective, the circular carousel should be at least 75% full.

- height adjustable feet;
- forward and reverse slide changing;
- spare bulb/s.

Our global sales for last year were ...

Our global markets are responding well ...

Optional extras that you may find useful:

- a slide previewer so that you can see what is coming up;
- automatic focusing as an override option;
- a light box to view slides when preparing the presentation;
- a carrying case, storage box or pocket files for the slides;
- a portable slide viewer for small presentations;
- an adjustable projector stand;
- a slide sorter such as that produced by Nobo – a translucent board that sits on a lightbox to arrange 35mm slides in order.

There are many slide projectors on the market from such manufacturers as Nobo, Sasco and AVP.

Some professional presenters reckon that it takes ten times as long to prepare for a successful speech as it takes to deliver it. Don't try to cut corners. Follow the four steps to a successful presentation:

step 1: research your material;

step 2: sort what you want to leave in and leave out;

step 3: build up your key points;

step 4: rehearse, not just once or twice, but at least three times.

"If your slides are the central focus of your presentation, the screen should be placed centre stage. But if your slides are supportive to you, and you want the attention on you it is better to have it to one side."

Cristina Stuart, SpeakEasy Training

SCREENS

There are a wide variety of projector screens available. In terms of white surface, there is little to choose between them. Your choice ultimately will come down to the budget you have and the special features offered by the screen. These may include:

- **size** – is the screen big enough to hold the entire slide image and still be seen clearly?

- **portability** – how quickly, easily and neatly can it be folded?

- **stability** – if it is free standing, how is it held up?

- **ease of use** – is it simple to put up without fuss or fiddly parts?

- **ability to angle the screen** – can it be tilted to avoid distortion caused by the "keystone effect"?

The keystone effect Increasing the angle of the projector head to give the image enough height can lead to distortion. This creates a wedge-shaped image which widens out towards the top of the screen. This "keystone effect" can be eliminated by tilting the screen, that is by bringing the top forward so that it stands at right angles to the beam.

Wall-mounted screens – simple pull-down screens usually in a fixed position.
Desktop screens – smaller models ideal for informal or small gatherings.
Portable screens without tripod legs – new designs of OHP are always being introduced. One is the Deltascreen which sits on its barrel casing supported by an extendable arm.
Electric screens – raised and lowered by an electric motor.

Phrases that are guaranteed to get your audience's back up. Never:
- apologise to your audience – "I am sorry if this seems long ....."
- congratulate yourself – "Well, of course without my involvement ..."
- fish for compliments – "I hope I have covered what you expected today."
- act subserviently – "I know that there are more knowledgeable people here today."
- tell them what you are not going to do – "I will not be discussing ...".

"If the room is darkened for a 35mm slide presentation you should stand at the front where your audience can see you. Use a small spotlight to focus the attention on you. Make sure the light does not come up from below because it may make you look like Dracula! A light is also important to enable you to see your notes."
Cristina Stuart, SpeakEasy Training

CREATING EXCITING VISUALS

35mm slides are particularly good for showing colour photographs and graphics. If your original material is in black and white, consider using an OHP transparency instead.

Avoid cramming too much information into one slide. The general rules about OHP transparencies are also applicable here:

- Keep your words large enough to be seen.
- Limit the number of lines per slide – as a general rule there should be no more than 14 lines of text per slide.
- Use simple, clear typefaces.
- Avoid the overuse of capital letters.
- Use visuals rather than text wherever possible.
- Use colour but don't abuse it – keep to around 4 colours if you are using your own graphics and make sure that the contrasts work well.

Colours that work well together

To be effective, your colour choice should emphasise the main text or graphic, provide a restful background and allow for effective highlighting. Here are some colour combinations that work well.

TABLE 5.1 Good colour combinations

Background	Text/graphic	Highlight
Blue	White, yellow	Magenta, black
Light blue	White, black, yellow	Yellow, white, black
Grey	Magenta, dark blue, yellow	Yellow, blue, crimson, green
Green	White, black	Crimson, white, black
White	Black, magenta, dark blue	Yellow, blue, crimson, green

If you want to win an audience over to your side, you must find out what their primary motives are. Is it power, prestige or recognition that they are looking for? Or security, trust, and reliability? Consider what the motivations are first, then work into your presentation benefits that will appeal to those motives.

HOW DO I PRODUCE MY OWN SLIDES?

It is relatively easy to produce effective 35mm colour slides of people and places, provided that you have a good 35mm camera. It is less easy to produce a good copy of, say, a company logo, text, graphics or other visuals which you have created. For this you need a good lighting system and a tripod-fixed camera that can get close in to your subject without losing sharp focus. Focus is all important here.

"When you are in the dark giving a 35mm slide presentation, you should remember that your voice can sound disembodied. Think carefully how you use your voice; you should aim to inject much more colour in it, more highs and lows and slow down the delivery. In highly illustrative 35mm slide presentations you are much more of a commentator than a speaker."

Cristina Stuart, SpeakEasy Training

HOW DO I LOOK AFTER MY SLIDES?

You may need to use your slides for presentations over many months or even years – it is advisable and relatively straightforward to look after them. Follow these simple rules:

1. Keep your fingers off them to avoid blurred patches.
2. Store your slides in a cool, well-ventilated room – slides can be harmed by damp or excessive heat.
3. Use glass-mounted slides as these do not distort with the heat from the projector.
4. Do not leave slides in your car overnight as condensation may form between the glass layers.
5. Keep a properly indexed library system of your slides so that you can get at them as and when they are needed.

Audiences invariably switch off at the sound of numbers. Find alternative ways of expressing them. Instead of sales of £400,000, try saying "an average couple will spend £50 a week. There are 4000 houses in Harworth village. That means we have attracted new customers equivalent to the size of two villages the size of Harworth in the past year. At that rate, in two years' time we will have attracted a whole town the size of Burnington as additional customers."

HOW DO I GIVE A SLIDE PRESENTATION?

Be prepared!

Before the presentation:

> Always pre-load the slide magazine – never load up during the presentation.

☐ Use a lightbox to help you decide which slides to use – the lightbox is a convenient way of displaying several slides at once.

☐ Check that the slides are in the correct order and loaded the right way up – this may take some practice.

☐ Ensure that the room is sufficiently darkened.

☐ Have plenty of blank slides at the ready to insert between slides you want to show. This saves the audience having to look at a glaringly bright but blank screen when you are between slides.

☐ Adjust the projector to the right height and level for the screen.

☐ Once you have loaded the slides into the carousel, seal it with tape to avoid them falling out in transit.

☐ Rehearse putting the slides into the carousel if you have to do that during the presentation.

☐ Number the slides in order of presentation (very useful if you drop them just before the event!).

If possible, quickly run through the slides to see if you have placed them in the correct order.

☐ If someone else is operating the slide projector for you, make sure that you go through the sequence with them to familiarise them with the material.

☐ If you are going to need a slide twice, make a copy of it – do not be tempted to take the original slide out and re-insert it.

☐ Have a second magazine ready loaded if you want to show more slides than the machine can handle at one time.

☐ Be prepared if a slide sticks – do you leave it and go on or try to go back to it?

An audience often likes to know where it is going. Unless you want to surprise them, consider issuing your handouts at the beginning. They can use them to add notes as you present which can increase their comprehension about what you are saying. The downside is that they may look at their handouts and not you. Think about the context and if it is appropriate.

Lighting

Unlike an OHP presentation, slide projection needs a fairly dark room but this means that you won't be seen! The best solution is to darken the room and have a separate spotlight on you. The other solution is to show your slides in groups – after each one you can turn the main lights back on for discussion.

We now have to decide which way to go ...

The road ahead may be tricky ...

We must avoid going round in circles ...

Giving the presentation: good techniques

These may take a little practice, but good technique really shows. Slide presentations that are ill conceived or badly rehearsed may do more harm than good – keep these tips in mind when you are delivering your slide presentation.

CHECKLIST – Tips for a skilful slide presentation

- ☐ Stand in front of the audience at all times – don't turn your back on them to talk to the screen.
- ☐ Don't disappear into the gloom, standing by the projector for instance. A disembodied voice is very hard to treat seriously.
- ☐ Check that you are not standing between the screen and the projector – thus creating offputting shadows.
- ☐ Keep your eyes on the audience as the slide changes – nervous glances to check on the screen hardly give the impression of authority.
- ☐ Use a pointer to highlight specific parts of the slide – don't wave it around like a nervous conductor.
- ☐ Leave the slides in long enough for the audience to take them in – keeping a slide on for twice as long as it takes to read it is a useful rule of thumb.
- ☐ When you have finished with a slide use a blank to return attention back to you.
- ☐ Have a blank slide ready for the end of the presentation so that you do not leave your audience gazing at a glaringly brilliant blank screen.

Video presentations –

sound and motion for a super-strong message

 "The best way to use a video is to show a clip and then pause it; get people to comment on what they have just seen or (in a training context) ask them if they have experienced something similar and get them to talk about the issues that have affected them. The video is then used as a device to spark off that discussion."
Catherine de Salvo, Fenman Training

GET TO KNOW YOUR EQUIPMENT

To show a video-based presentation, you will need:

- a video playback machine;

- a television monitor;

- your videotape;

- a remote control system.

There are many brands of video playback machine on the market. For the best and simplest effects you will need one that allows:

- **freeze frame** – the ability to stop the programme at any point;

- **a review facility** when rewinding and fast forwarding – this enables you to watch the programme in a speeded-up version;

- **a counter** that can be set to help find your place in the programme;

- **a fully functioning remote control panel** – that allows you to switch on and off, alter the volume, colour, brightness and contrast settings, freeze frame, cue and review (see "review facility" above).

It is most important that you have all the key controls at your fingertips – you do not want to be scrambling around trying to work out the function of all the small knobs and buttons on the player.

We are not going to
make any U turns ...

There is only one
way for all of us ...

PREPARATION BEFORE USING A VIDEO

- Make sure that you know how the machine works before the presentation. Models differ in how they operate. Get to know the one you will be using and make sure that all necessary connections are made between the monitor and the player.

- Make sure that the videotape and the player are compatible. You cannot, for instance, show Betamax videos on VHS machines. You cannot play videos from the USA on British machines. Video programmes recorded at double speed will not play on single speed machines.

- Do not use more than one videotape during a presentation unless there is a sufficient gap between them. It is boring for the audience to watch someone changing the tape over.

- Unless the programme has been specially commissioned for your purposes, watch it carefully and ensure that every part you intend to show has some relevance. There is nothing worse than a presenter telling an audience, "I'm sorry, a lot of this is irrelevant but you'll find one or two useful points." In this case it is much better either to show only the relevant sections of the programme or to present the material in a different way.

Never use a script to give your presentation. It makes you sound stiff and stilted and stops you using eye contact to draw your audience's attention. Prompt cards listing key words will help you maintain the flow and keep it sounding natural.

VIDEO DOS AND DON'TS

✗ Don't use a video just as entertainment. Ask yourself, "What is this video for? Is it really the best way of presenting this material?"

✗ Don't rely on a normal television screen for a group that is any larger than 20 people. Above this number use a video projector or a number of TV screens, or don't use a video.

✗ Don't run a section for more than 15–20 minutes – more than this and your audience can become mesmerised, making it very difficult to get their attention back.

✗ Don't use videos that just show "talking heads", i.e. static images of people talking. Many "home made" corporate videos have been produced as an ego boost for the chief executive. People would much rather be addressed by a live person than a television image. Only use video where it involves movement.

✓ Be very careful about finding your place in the programme. Audiences quickly get bored with presenters who are forever fast forwarding or rewinding the tape trying to find the place or muttering, "It's here somewhere".

✓ Before the presentation, make sure that you know precisely how the video works.

 "I have seen some terrible presentations where the video wasn't in the right place or the person wasn't properly prepared to use it. Many people use the video just as an excuse for a break. To get the most from a video it should illustrate the message you are trying to get across."

Catherine de Salvo, Fenman Training

POSITIONING THE VIDEO

For a larger audience, video can be shown on a series of monitors placed around the room. If the budget allows, you can also buy special video projectors which utilise a large screen.

With an audience of under 15 or so, you can use an ordinary television screen but check carefully that the picture is clear for everyone and the volume is set at the right level.

If you are using a normal television monitor, you may have to consider darkening the room if there is a lot of outside light. This can be a problem if you want to interact with the programme. Another complication is that many people resent having their TV programme interrupted. It may be advisable to show a segment of the video without interruption.

A voice that drones will not keep an audience awake. Vary the pitch, change the volume and add short dramatic pauses to enliven your voice. Questions (both rhetorical and those put to an audience) will force you to change your tone.

HOW DO I MAKE THE MOST OF A VIDEO PRESENTATION?

Videos that work

Video programmes tend to come from one of three sources:

1. "Off the shelf" from a professional video training company. These may be bought or hired. There are few business and management subjects not covered by the wealth of videos now available.

2. Videos commissioned by your organisation and professionally produced.

3. Videos that have been made by you using a portable video camera.

> The more that the video has been tailored to your needs, the easier and more relevant it will be to use.

Videos that are made by amateurs need very careful handling. They are all too often rather static and involve people talking to camera: something you could be doing much more effectively "live".

Videos that have been commercially produced for purchase or hire may well be excellent and just the thing you need. However, the chances that all of the programme will be relevant are rather slim. All videos should be treated with caution. To make sure that they are relevant to your needs follow the advice below:

☐ Watch the programme at least twice, make careful notes about its content and style (you may find that the programme is accompanied by printed notes that provide a synopsis of the scenes).

☐ Think carefully about how the programme can assist your presentation. It may do this by illustrating a case, showing an example of what you are talking about, using moving graphics that you could not otherwise show, interviewing key people, giving useful historical background and so on.

☐ Do not show any sequence for more than 20 minutes without some kind of feedback. Any longer than this tends to mesmerise an audience, making it very difficult to recapture their attention.

Always allow for the unexpected to happen. If you are waiting for a speaker to turn up who is late, keep a nice surprise up your sleeve to fill the gap – such as an informal friendly quiz to keep the participants actively interested or a spare video clip to use in an instructional way.

 "It is no good just showing a video clip and then asking your audience if there are any questions. That is not a very interesting way to show a video – it is just like showing a programme. People won't remember very much and it will just wash over them. To make a video presentation work you have got to get people to engage in what they have seen."

Catherine de Salvo, Fenman Training

Finding your place in the video

- Unless the programme uses an on-screen timer, use a video player with a counter.
- Set the counter to zero and make sure that the videotape is fully rewound.
- Before the presentation, make sure that all your cues are numbered so that you can go quickly to the right place in the video.
- Use a remote control device to fast forward, rewind or pause – there is nothing more offputting than to see a presenter bent double trying to fiddle with the tiny knobs and buttons of the video player.

If at all possible, try to avoid skipping around the videotape. Fast forwarding or rewinding can take time, it demands your attention and it inevitably means an embarassing pause in the proceedings. If you have to do this, consider giving the audience a short break before moving to another part of the tape. Alternatively, if this is possible and allowable, edit the video so that the running order corresponds to your needs. Given enough rehearsal and preferably with an assistant, you could fast forward and so on as you introduce the next topic. The main aim here is not to interrupt the flow by having to work the machine.

CHECKLIST – preparing to use a video

- ☐ I am sure that the programme is relevant to my needs.
- ☐ I have seen the programme and have incorporated it into my presentation.
- ☐ I know how the player, TV screen and remote control device work.
- ☐ The video is fully rewound or set to the part of the programme I want to show.
- ☐ I have set the volume and colour contrast before the presentation begins.
- ☐ I am sure that every member of the audience will be able to see and hear the programme.

Part Two

Presentation know-how – ensuring everything is all right on the night

This part explains how to prepare for the presentation, what to do on the day and how to deliver a strong impact. The advice will help you to prepare for and create a powerful presentation.

Three weeks to go –

7

plenty of time, but time to make a start

"Successful presentation is one-tenth inspiration, nine-tenths preparation."
So says an experienced business presenter who has seen it all – from simple
factual presentations for small and informal groups of fellow managers to
glossy marketing exercises before large audiences of yet-to-be-convinced
customers.

Whatever kind of presentation you envisage, the key to its success lies in
careful planning beforehand. Getting the groundwork right can make all the
difference between a sparky presentation that will stay long in the memory,
and a dull, slapdash affair that is best forgotten in a hurry.

The key to good planning lies in knowing exactly what you want the
presentation to achieve. This means asking some basic questions:

- What message do I want to deliver?

- Who is my audience?

- What do they already know?

- How large is the audience?

- Where will the presentation take place?

- How long will it last?

- How do I start?

- What result do I want?

Let's take each of these questions in turn.

Learn your very first few lines (but not your whole speech) – your start will be
more confident, you will not be lost for words and you will find the rest of your
speech goes much more smoothly.

"A useful ice-breaker that I use is to get each person in turn to say who they are and what they hope to get out of the day. This immediately opens an audience up and helps them to become more involved in the presentation."

David Martin, Buddenbrook Consultancy

WHAT MESSAGE DO I WANT TO DELIVER?

Before you plan your presentation, think carefully about the message you want to deliver.

What are the essential points? List these and make sure that they appear in the presentation in order of priority. These essential points, and there may only be two or three, are the ones that you want the audience to remember above all else.

In addition to the essential points, you will probably want to include some non-essential material that is still important but in a supporting role.

A third category of information may be there to illustrate a point or add some light relief. Most people enjoy personal anecdotes, humorous stories that support your main points or something local or topical. Always try to include some of this lighter material for your audience to enjoy.

Graphic ideas

You must be prepared to sail closer to the wind ...

We must be first past the post ...

Guidelines

Here are some useful guidelines for preparing your message:

1. Make a draft of your entire presentation, including all essential, non-essential and anecdotal points.
2. Rehearse the presentation and look out for key words and phrases – highlight these in the text.
3. See if you can present the information just by using the key words.
4. Transfer these key words to a series of prompt cards.
5. Keep on reducing your message down to its barest essentials.

Four ways to hook your audience and make them want to listen on:

- Create an image in their minds – "Imagine if we only had to work at weekends and had five days off...."

- Give them an alternative to consider – "Cutting costs or raising expenditure".

- Ask them to write down the first thing they think about when you mention the word success (or the topic under discussion). Then list them on a flipchart.

- Create a sketch related to the subject to be acted out by two or three colleagues. This can be particularly good to explain a complicated process and will be very memorable.

WHO IS MY AUDIENCE?

The more you know about your audience, the better prepared you will be to make an effective presentation. Here are some key questions to ask while preparing your presentation:

Key questions

1. Who will be coming and what is their general level and status? If possible find out the names of those who will be there.
2. Are key decision makers going to be there? For example, those people who can act on my presentation?
3. Are all the potential decision makers and decision influencers going to be there?
4. What is the mood of the audience likely to be when I arrive? For example, what has happened before the presentation? What are their usual preferences in terms of style, content and length? How receptive will they be? Are they willing participants or is attendance compulsory?

To explain complex information to your audience, don't throw it at them all at once. You will only confuse them and not win anyone over to your side. Break it down into a series of steps or put it into a flow chart. Reveal the explanation step by step until the complete picture has been built up.

 "One of the most effective techniques that I have used to grab people's attention is to fire a gun (but not a real one) at the beginning of the presentation. This presentation concerned writing effective reports. The message I wanted to convey was that reports should be short, sharp and capture attention. The gun being fired achieved this very well. You must be careful though – a tactic like this must fit the occasion and the audience."

David Martin, Buddenbrook Consultancy

WHAT DO THEY ALREADY KNOW?

One of the keys to successful presentation is to put yourself in the audience's shoes. Every time you make a presentation, ask yourself, "how will the audience see my point of view? What expectations do they have?".

By knowing as much as possible about your audience in advance, you will be better prepared either to match their expectations or to surprise them in some deliberate way.

What do the audience know about you and your subject? The more you know about this aspect of your audience, the more ready you will be to catch their mood, level and likely response to your presentation. The less they know, the more background material you may have to provide. A well-briefed audience will require little introduction to the subject save a cursory summary of the main points to get them into the central ideas behind your presentation.

If you don't know what to do with your hands when you are standing up in front of an audience try holding some prompt cards in a relaxed way. Don't grip on to them for dear life. Occasionally putting your hands in your pockets can send them an "I'm feeling relaxed signal" but watch out you don't rattle your keys. Use them naturally to gesture and add emphasis to your presentation.

The level and sophistication of the audience will also determine the speed of your delivery.

Be prepared to slow down if:

● you naturally talk fast;

● you are nervous;

● your audience may contain people with different levels of understanding;

● the topic is new to most people in the audience and contains some technical material;

● there are people in the audience whose first language is not English;

● you have a strong dialect or accent which may be difficult for others to understand.

The best way to find out the strengths and weaknesses in your presentation is to ask a friend to listen to your delivery and give an honest view.

   "To break the ice with a large audience ask them a question. For example, if you were talking about public transport you could ask them the question: how many of you came by bus today?"
Cristina Stuart, SpeakEasy Training

HOW LARGE IS THE AUDIENCE?

The size of your prospective audience will affect how you present to them and which aids you use. Here are some useful rules of thumb:

Rules of thumb

Small group – usually under 10 people

This audience size is ideal for the informal, one-to-one approach in which relationships need to be made quickly. Consider using a desktop flipchart and sit with the group around a table. See the presentation more as an informed discussion led by you towards your objective.

Medium-sized group – 10 to 30 people

With this size you may need to be more formal in your approach. Stand up and use larger visual aid formats such as an easel or wall-mounted flipcharts, overhead projector transparencies, whiteboards. This size of group is ideal for interactive sessions where questions, answers and opinions flow freely.

Large group – 30 to 100 people

Less easy to establish a personal rapport with your audience. Use large-scale aids such as slide projectors and overhead projectors. You may also need to use a microphone.

Extra-large group – over 100 people

Consider very carefully how you will be seen and heard. Seating may have to be raked so that people at the back can see you. Use a large screen format to project slides and transparencies, a microphone, and stage lighting which focuses on you and your message.

"I won't plan to make an audience laugh before a presentation because I am not a comic and don't feel confident enough to make them laugh. If it happens naturally then that is fine but I would not engineer it. If it is forced there is a big danger that it can fall flat on its face."

Catherine de Salvo, Fenman Training

We must be on
our guard ...

The danger for
our business is ...

WHERE WILL THE PRESENTATION TAKE PLACE?

The venue for your presentation can be a crucial factor in its success. Where possible, try to see a venue before you present in it for the first time. If this is not possible, ask to see a ground plan of the space including entrances, exits, screen areas, seating layout and so on.

Try to ensure that the room is welcoming and makes a good first impression. Use the venue checklist below to make sure that everything will be right.

CHECKLIST – is the venue suitable?

- ☐ Is the seating comfortable?
- ☐ Will the people at the back see clearly?
- ☐ Is the room well lit?
- ☐ Are the acoustics good?
- ☐ Can I control heating and/or air conditioning?
- ☐ Will the first impression of the room be a good one?
- ☐ Will the right equipment be in place for my presentation?
- ☐ Will the external environment be quiet?
- ☐ Will there be any interruptions during the presentation (e.g. from catering staff)?
- ☐ Will the audience be properly welcomed and directed to the room?

Don't treat an accident as a disaster. Look for the amusing quip to turn it on its head and break down the barrier between yourself and your audience and relieve tension on both sides. If you trip and fall in front of your audience, try saying something like: "It seems someone up there doesn't want me to speak to you down here. I just hope he can wait half an hour."

HOW LONG WILL IT LAST?

The length of your presentation can be crucial to its success. Many potentially excellent presentations have reduced their impact by running on too long. The result can be a tired or bored audience, an exhausted presenter, and an irate venue manager who has to juggle the rest of the day's events.

While the length of your presentation may be determined to some extent by your host and/or the amount of material you want to get through, remember these golden rules about timing.

- Rehearse your presentation so that it will comfortably fit into the time available – make sure that the key points are covered.
- Don't waste time by unnecessary waffle at the beginning – get straight to the point and never begin with an apology ("I'm sorry I haven't got more time for this" or worse, "I've not had time to prepare this talk properly").
- Allow extra time for questions at the end.
- Remember that most presentations are too long – go for brevity, the shorter the better.
- Recognise the value of your audience's time by telling them at the start how long you will take and what time they can expect to get away.

The golden rules of phrasing:

- Keep it simple.
- Keep sentences short (no more than 10 to 15 words).
- Avoid unnecessary jargon.

HOW DO I START?

It is useful to start your presentation with some general points which set the right tone, yet which do not deny latecomers any vital information.

Your preface may include:

- a very short welcome thanking people for coming and hoping that they will find the presentation useful and interesting;
- a short explanation of who you are (if you are not already known to the audience) and why you are the right person to give this talk;
- a brief outline of the purpose of the presentation;
- a very brief outline of the structure of the presentation explaining:
  - when it will finish;
  - if there is to be a break;
  - when questions will be encouraged.

Be original in your opening. Avoid the well-worn and over-used phrases such as "Ladies and Gentlemen…" Try to add suspense or even a little drama. "Today we are all going to commit a murder. (Pause.) … We are going to kill an outdated method of working….."

WHAT RESULT DO I WANT?

In some ways this is the most important part of getting the groundwork right: what do you hope to achieve as a result of your presentation? The last thing you want is for people to say "very interesting" but then take no action.

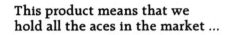

This product means that we hold all the aces in the market ...

There is only one king in this business – our customers.

This means thinking clearly about your purpose in giving the presentation. Concentrate your mind here by writing down your objectives in no more than fifteen words. Examples might be:

"To persuade each salesperson to make one extra appointment a day with a customer."
or
"To win the new order."
or
"To persuade the directors to accept my proposal."

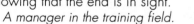

"I keep a watch handy to ensure that I do not go over time. It is essential to keep the uninterrupted time to no more than 25 minutes or half an hour at most. Beyond this, most people's attention starts to wander. If the subject is one that takes more than this time, I would consider splitting the presentation into two or more parts with a break in between. I always tell my audience when the last ten minutes are about to begin – this helps them to concentrate fully knowing that the end is in sight."
A manager in the training field.

Your ending is the most important part of your presentation when your audience will be at their most alert. Deliver your key message at this point – the one you want them to go away with, but don't spring it on them. Signal to them that the end is near by saying "And finally...".

There is no need to make your objective too verbose – try to encapsulate it in as few words as possible, which will help you to get to the root of what your presentation is for.

Once you know who your audience will be, you can assess in advance whether the objectives set are achievable. If, for instance, relevant key decision makers are not coming, you may have to consider changing the objectives of the presentation (or postponing it).

When you are clear about the results you want to achieve, you can plan how to tackle the presentation to achieve your desired result.

> When you have planned the contents of the presentation, go back and check that you have met your objectives. Be prepared to work on some of the material again to bring it up to scratch.

CHECKLIST – getting the key points right

Complete this checklist before every presentation:

- [ ] I know what I want the presentation to achieve.
- [ ] All the essential points are included in my notes.
- [ ] I have rehearsed my presentation more than once.
- [ ] I have found out what I can about the audience.
- [ ] I know the size of the audience and have planned my visual aids accordingly.
- [ ] I have checked the venue.
- [ ] I know how long the presentation will last.

Two weeks to go –

structure, story and variety

8

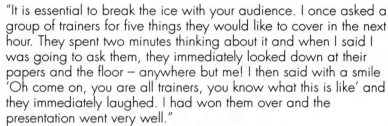

"It is essential to break the ice with your audience. I once asked a group of trainers for five things they would like to cover in the next hour. They spent two minutes thinking about it and when I said I was going to ask them, they immediately looked down at their papers and the floor – anywhere but me! I then said with a smile 'Oh come on, you are all trainers, you know what this is like' and they immediately laughed. I had won them over and the presentation went very well."

Catherine de Salvo, Fenman Training

GATHER YOUR MATERIALS TOGETHER

As a presenter your job is to deliver your material in the most interesting and stimulating way. You must organise your material in a way that forms a seamless bond between what you say and what you show. This takes practice and organisation and a clear idea of how each element of your presentation fits together: the script, the visual aids and any samples shown.

The first stage in preparing for your presentation is to gather all your materials together.

What do you want to say?

The centrepiece of the event will be what you are going to say. This should be well planned: only the rarest individuals are able to speak effectively off the cuff. What you are going to say should be put into an outline which will serve as the structure for the presentation. This should not appear as a word for word text – you will not come across naturally to the audience and will be unable to maintain eye contact with them. The best outlines are those that give you (a) the key words which will spark the ideas you want to project, and (b) a list of the visual aids giving details of when to show them and in what order.

Think about ways of getting your audience to participate actively. Arrange a friendly quiz or get them to complete a self-test questionnaire, saying what they can learn from it afterwords.

A framework for writing an effective outline

1. Write in rough note form all the points you want to make. At this stage, do not exclude any items.
2. Put the notes in order. Although every presentation is different, most follow part or all of this sequence of events:
   (a) **Setting the scene.** Why is the audience here? What is your goal? What is their goal? What is the common ground between you? How were things in the past? What has been achieved since that time?
   (b) **Developing the theme.** For example, is there a problem that you can help to clarify or solve? Why must changes be made? What is the new direction? What will be important for the future?
   (c) **Possible courses of action.** The pros and cons of different alternatives.
   (d) **What you would recommend.** Your proposals, backed by a strong argument.
   (e) **A summary or conclusion.** Reiterate your points and make sure the key message that you want to leave with the audience is reiterated. For example, a recommended course of action: "If we take this road, everyone will benefit because..."
   (f) **General thanks.** Make sure you don't exclude anyone who should be thanked.
   (g) **Session for questions.** Be prepared to answer questions and consider in advance the kinds of questions that might be put to you.

Fill your presentation with relevant examples to illustrate the points you are making. Instead of saying "10 per cent of our customers have not renewed their orders" say, "There are 30 people in this room. Imagine ten times that number. That is the number of people we have lost as customers since the beginning of this year."

"One of the best ways to inject enthusiasm and charisma into your presentation is to know your subject really well. Prepare, prepare and prepare are the three essential watchwords."
David Martin, Buddenbrook Consultancy

DECIDING WHAT TO USE

Once you have written out your notes, look at the contents very carefully. There are bound to be points which can be cut. Think through carefully what you want your key message to be and stick to it. Don't try to pack in too many messages. Most presentations are far too long. Divide your notes into three categories:

- essential;
- desirable;
- unnecessary.

Essential. Points that will support your key message.
Desirable. These items are not essential to your core message but they do reinforce points that you are making.
Unnecessary. These are points that are tangential to the core message. This category can be hard to cut as you may think the point is nevertheless important. You will have to be ruthless. Your audience will not thank you for an over-long presentation, and remember, no speaker has ever been criticised for being too short!

If you have any doubts about some ideas in your notes, cut them out. Remember that short is sweet!

Now do the same thing with your visual aids. Divide them into:

- essential;
- desirable;
- unnecessary.

Cut out anything that is there just for the ride.

Once you have decided which materials and notes are essential, you can start putting them in order. Rearrange your notes into a workable outline, i.e. one that you can easily follow once you are on your feet in front of an audience.

Then mark up where the visual aids will fit into your delivery.

To end on a high note and keep your audience motivated offer your audience a vision of the future. Make it realistic and achievable. "If we maintain progress at the same rate, in three years' time we shall grow to a division the size of our sister company."

"Don't ignore an audience that is not paying attention to you. The natural reaction of some speakers can be to speed up and get through it as quickly as possible because the audience are bored. Instead, stop and find out what is not interesting and adjust your presentation accordingly."

Cristina Stuart, SpeakEasy Training

LOOK FOR A STORY

Your presentation should be telling a good story – one that will keep your audience really involved and interested. Try it out. Rehearse the presentation, in front of colleagues if possible.

The elements of a good story

Your presentation should never just consist of a list of facts and figures. This will be very boring for the audience and they are unlikely to concentrate on your message. Wherever possible, turn your presentation into a story incorporating all the facts and figures they need.

1. **A good story should be personal** – "I first got involved in this market in 1991, imagine how I felt when..." or "We were faced with a problem of declining sales and increased competition – what should we do?"

2. **Involve narrative** – an ordered storyline which begs the question "And what happened next?"

3. **Create a clear beginning, middle and end** – like any good story, make sure that your presentation has this structure.

    Beginning. Why this presentation is so useful/interesting/relevant to you today. Where possible try to begin with a memorable opening – something that will grab the attention. For example, "Ladies and gentlemen, I want to begin by announcing a death – from today complacency is dead."

    Middle. For example handling conflicts and problems in reaching a desired goal. "So now we know the problems, how do we solve them, given the practical problems of..."

    End. How it is all going to end happily. Summarise your presentation and end on a memorable note such as: "And as you see, ladies and gentlemen, today could be the most important day of your life – the day when you decide finally that change is coming. From today your lives are not going to be the same."

4. **Use your own personal experience** – stories that have involved you personally will come across much more convincingly than ones that you have picked up third hand. They can be very effective in illustrating and enlivening the presentation.

5. **Use humour (but don't force it)** – even the most serious issues can be dealt with in a relaxed and friendly way. Remember that your chief objective as a presenter is to communicate with your audience, not just to give a list of facts. If you are not certain that what you are saying will be amusing, try it out on friends or colleagues – they will soon let you know. If you are at all uncertain, it is safer to leave it out.

If you want to inject some humour stick to one-liners. If it doesn't work you can move on without affecting your presentation.

"Most people don't realise how little eye contact they give. The more stressful the situation, the more difficult it can be to concentrate on the listeners. The person who is looking most friendly often gets all the eye contact. You should look at everyone."

Cristina Stuart, SpeakEasy Training

SHOULD I USE A SCRIPT?

The answer to this is "definitely not". A script will come in between you and your audience. Remember, it is important that you maintain eye contact with your audience. The last thing people want to see is your nose buried in a script. Reading a word-for-word script also ties you down to a very rigid delivery where you are unable to adapt what you say to the mood and unique atmosphere of your audience on the day. Your delivery should be natural: reading from a script will make it stilted.

It is far better to use main headings and notes written on little prompt cards like the one illustrated in Figure 9.1.

Don't be afraid to use these cards as prompts but don't be seen to be clutching on to them for dear life. Some presenters like to cup the relevant card in the palm of their hand so that it becomes an extension of their arm as you use hand gestures and arm movements, you can casually glance at the card without having to study it too closely.

Key reasons for our success last year:

*   Steady market growth – we estimated 3% but the outcome was 6%
*   Market share leapt – 26% to 31%: how?

> – better marketing in Midlands
> – supply problems sorted out at Northants depot
> – launch of the Premiere range

Figure 9.1 A prompt card

Alternatives to using card prompts

If you want to present some detailed facts in conjunction with an OHP, don't put everything onto your prompt card. Use a card mount or Flip-Frame™ for your OHP.

Then write pencil notes on the card mounts used with your OHP transparencies. Alternatively using an aid such as 3M's Flip-Frame™ you can write on the opaque margins on each side of the transparency.

If you are using a flipchart, write notes in light pencil or a yellow marker: neither will be seen by an audience.

"If there's some important fact I want to mention at that point, I write it in pencil on the card mount the audience are usually very impressed by my apparently phenomenal memory."
Training manager in a large multinational

KEEP IT SHORT AND SIMPLE

There is a very useful acronym you should remember when preparing for presentations: KISS, standing for keep it short and simple.

Short

Short is good. It is unlikely that people will remember more than seven things told to them at any one session. Do not cram lots of facts and ideas into one presentation. Also, do not talk for more than 25 minutes. Any longer is counter-productive.

Simple

Keeping it simple is vital if your audience can follow your argument clearly and simply, they are much more likely to empathise with your message. Never try to hoodwink or bamboozle an audience. They will not think you clever, merely irrelevant. Even if the information you have to deliver is itself complex, you must make it simple for your audience. Don't assume they will have the same level of comprehension as you. If possible use analogies or examples to explain complex ideas.

If your mouth dries up in the middle of a speech and the organisers have forgotten to put any water out, gently bite your tongue which helps to generate saliva.

LOOK FOR WAYS OF ADDING VARIETY

The more variety you can include in your presentation, the more lively, interesting and memorable it is likely to be.

You can add variety in your verbal presentation by using:

- anecdotes;
- definitions;
- facts;
- metaphor;
- questions;

- data;
- examples;
- humour;
- opinion;
- quotes.

Add variety in your visual presentation by showing:

- key bullet points;
- charts;

- graphs;
- cartoons and other illustrations.

Add variety to your overall presentation by using:

- speech;
- OHP transparencies for prepared visuals;
- flipcharts for adding the views of the audience;
- colour in your visuals.

 Don't use jokes on an audience; it requires them to respond actively to what has been said and will be immediately apparent if it is a flop.

HOW WHAT YOU SAY INTERACTS WITH YOUR VISUAL AIDS

However good your visual aids, you are still the most important element of the presentation. Remember, the visuals are there to support what you say and not the other way round.

This means that you should carefully rehearse the balance between you and your visuals. Here are some useful tips:

How to achieve a seamless presentation with your visual aids

1. Using your card prompts and the visuals, rehearse your presentation so that you know when to introduce the next slide.

2. Check that the visual and what you have said do not contradict each other or say the same thing. The visual is there as food for thought, as an audience prompt. For example, "As you can see from this slide, the first problem is..."

3. Make sure that you can operate the technology with ease and confidence so that there is no embarrassing pause between what you say and what you show but...

4. ...do not be afraid of silences. You can use the time taken to put on the next transparency as a dramatic pause: "You are about to see something that may surprise or even shock..."

5. Use a pointer to emphasise particular words or data, or use a reveal method, where you gradually unmask a point that you want to speak about.

6. Using visuals can help you stay in control of a presentation.

"When I'm using an OHP transparency, I often cover part of the acetate with ordinary 80gsm photocopy paper. This is thin enough to see through when the light from the OHP is switched on but the audience can't see it up on screen. In this way, the transparency tells me which point is coming next and I can structure my talk accordingly."

Manager of a major retailer

Moving on
"If we have questions during the presentation but I feel that enough time has been spent on it, I put up the next slide or transparency, or write something on the flipchart. This immediately stops the audience and signals that you have moved on."

A management trainer

If you suddenly get stuck in your presentation and can't remember the point you were going to make:

- leave it out and move on to the next point (no one will notice);

- tell your audience you will come back to it later;

- invite questions on any points covered so far.

One week to go –

time to rehearse and gain feedback

   "If you forget what you were going to say next, simply pause. You could also invite your audience to comment on what has been said so far or ask your audience 'Where was I going with this? I seem to have forgotten what I was going to say.' Throw it open to them."

Cristina Stuart, SpeakEasy Training

We will assume that well before the presentation you have:
- worked on your script and reduced it down to its essential parts;
- chosen the means of delivery, i.e. which visual aids to use;
- chosen the venue (if this is down to you).

Assuming that this basic preparation is complete – you have one week to go, what is the best use of your time?

Here is a suggested list of things to do, and some advice on how to do them.

 You find yourself put on the spot in a presentation with a tricky question.

- Offer it to the rest of the audience for suggestions.

- Invite the questioner to come and discuss it with you after the session.

- Throw it back to the questioner asking them for their views on it.

- Say you don't know the answer and offer to find out the answer for them.

   "Humour is essential in a presentation. Laughter has the advantage of forcing your audience to draw in oxygen which immediately makes them more alert and helps them to focus their attention on you. Building a light-hearted comment around a topical event – something that has been in the news recently – can be very effective and it helps to break the ice with your audience and make them warm to you."

David Martin, Buddenbrook Consultancy

REHEARSALS

Every presenter, however experienced, should rehearse his or her piece before the event. Rehearsals are extremely valuable and should be taken very seriously. The purposes of rehearsals are:

- to test the effectiveness of your presentation;
- to familiarise yourself with the narrative to be used;
- to practise using your voice and appropriate body language;
- to help overcome nervousness and stress.

A rehearsal does not entail learning a script word for word – it does, however, mean becoming truly familiar with your subject matter and the materials you will be using (and the equipment that will be employed).

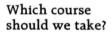

Which course should we take?	**We must penetrate all our markets more deeply**

How do I rehearse?

1. Read your presentation aloud, into a tape recorder or ideally to another person who can give you an encouraging, honest but critical opinion. Repeat the exercise two or three times.
2. From this experience decide which parts of the presentation to leave out and which to stress.
3. Decide if your planned use of visual aids will work.
4. Try to memorise certain fixed elements of the presentation – the welcome and introduction, any key facts that people would expect you to know, anecdotes and quotations, your conclusion.
5. Time your presentation carefully.

Presentations usually involve an audience's two basic senses of sight and sound. For an original and more enlivening experience which forces the audience to respond, why not design a presentation involving the other senses of touch, taste and smell? If you feel your topic does not lend itself to these senses in any way, design it as a deliberate break from the main theme of the event. It could be used to wake up an otherwise sleepy audience that has started to drop off.

FEEDBACK

It is essential that you get some kind of feedback to your rehearsal. This can be your own feedback, how you think the audience will respond, or preferably that of a test audience.

CHECKLIST – getting feedback from a test audience

Get your test audience to mark your presentation against the criteria listed below on a 1–5 scale, where 1 = poor, 2 = more work needed, 3 = satisfactory, 4 = good, 5 = excellent, etc. (Alternatively, mark yourself.)

Criteria	1	2	3	4	5
The introduction grabs the audience's attention	☐	☐	☐	☐	☐
The introduction helps to anticipate what is to come	☐	☐	☐	☐	☐
The purpose of the presentation is clear	☐	☐	☐	☐	☐
It is all easy to understand	☐	☐	☐	☐	☐
The ideas are explained clearly	☐	☐	☐	☐	☐
The language is pitched correctly for this audience	☐	☐	☐	☐	☐
It is interesting	☐	☐	☐	☐	☐
Information shown on visual aids is effective	☐	☐	☐	☐	☐
There is a smooth link between speaker and visual aids	☐	☐	☐	☐	☐
The visual aids are well designed	☐	☐	☐	☐	☐
Everything can be seen and heard clearly	☐	☐	☐	☐	☐
The speaker's delivery is pleasant and interesting	☐	☐	☐	☐	☐
The speaker doesn't seem to be waffling	☐	☐	☐	☐	☐
The speaker seems in control of his or her material	☐	☐	☐	☐	☐
The conclusion links all the parts together properly	☐	☐	☐	☐	☐
The amount of time seems right	☐	☐	☐	☐	☐

The best way of controlling nerves and stage-fright is to prepare thoroughly and well in advance of the event. By doing this, you will build up your confidence. Learn your start especially well. A good strong start will get you off the starting blocks and smooth the way for the rest of your presentation.

"At the end of seminar presentations I give, a questionnaire is handed to the participants asking them for their comments. This feedback is very useful for pointing out topics that may have been omitted. Some of the comments have to be taken with a pinch of salt though. The seminar organisers use the technique of ignoring all the 'excellent' and 'very poor' comments and gauging the result from the comments in the middle for judging the success of the day."
David Martin, Buddenbrook Consultancy.

THE DRESS REHEARSAL

Try to have a final rehearsal a day or two before the event. Where possible this should be in the actual venue under the same conditions that you will find in reality (ideally at the same time of day so that the light and sound conditions can be anticipated).

Practise with all the equipment until you are confident in using it without any worries. If you will be using an OHP, test your transparencies on the screen provided.

On the day – 10

making sure it all goes to plan

 "I find it very useful for handling nerves to talk to the individuals before the presentation over a cup of coffee. This makes me think they are real people and have ordinary concerns and families of their own. Individually they are lovely people and collectively they are just the same people. Just because they are part of a big audience doesn't change them."
Catherine de Salvo, Fenman Training

AVOID LAST MINUTE EMERGENCIES

One of the best ways of avoiding any last minute emergencies is to spend an hour or so before the presentation doing a last check and getting prepared.

✓ Have one more rehearsal in private.
✓ Make any final cuts necessary and err on the side of brevity.
✓ Be aware of the news that day – can you add anything that lends topical interest to your presentation?

Get to the venue with at least one hour to spare.

If it is a large presentation, make yourself known to the technical people and the venue organiser, check that everything is in place and that you will not be unexpectedly interrupted.

Find out what you can about your audience – if at all possible, meet some of them informally before the presentation.

If you have to give a presentation without a microphone and want to make sure everyone can hear you, imagine the room is half as long again as it really is and that you have to make someone right at the back hear, but beware of shouting. There is nothing more infuriating to an audience than not being able to hear a speaker.

CHECKLIST – just before you go on

☐ Does the room layout meet my needs? If not, can I rearrange the chairs and equipment?

☐ Are all sight lines clear? Nothing is blocking the view of me, the screen, the chart, the board or the TV monitor.

☐ All the equipment is working and I have test focused my OHP transparencies, slides and so on.

☐ I have checked that I can be heard and seen from the back.

"It is important to keep your audience informed if there is a technical fault which is holding up the event. As soon as people know, they are quite sympathetic and understanding. But you should have a contingency plan to fill the time if someone needs to find some replacement equipment."

Catherine de Salvo, Fenman Training

We may feel boxed in

All the ideas point to one solution ...

WHAT DO I DO IF A VISUAL AID GOES WRONG?

It happens to the best presenters: your last spare bulb blows, the room is too light, the video player provided is not compatible with your tape, the organisers have forgotten to provide a flipchart... Things are bound to go wrong one day – what do you do?

● **Don't panic** – remember that the audience will be even more nervous than you. Never be afraid to admit that things have gone wrong – try to carry it off with humour (and a little well-placed humility).

- **Always try to plan for an emergency** – what could you valuably do if the equipment or venue organisers let you down? Perhaps a simple talk – you could promise to give the main points to the audience in the form of a handout either later that day or in the near future. The more relaxed and able to cope with the crisis you are, the more the audience will respect your ability to offer alternatives.

- **Ask the audience to have a break for a few minutes** – this will give you valuable breathing space to get hold of the equipment you need or to rearrange the presentation.

- **Consider cancelling the presentation** – but only as a last resort.

Natural humour can gain an audience's attention and interest, but do not force it. The humour must be relevant to the audience and the context of the presentation.

THIRTY MINUTES BEFORE

This is the time to start getting mentally and physically prepared to give your presentation. Try not to do any of the checks mentioned above in this period – it will only make you panic if things are not right.

Relax

While some people find that being too relaxed can dull the edge of the presentation, you do want to go in there feeling in control, lively and ready to start. How do you relax?

✓ Do some relaxation exercises.

The simplest relaxation exercise is to close your eyes and breathe slowly and rhythmically, concentrating only on the sound of your breathing. Think of all those tense parts of your body the shoulders, the mouth, the jaw, the eyes and try consciously to relax these areas while you think of your breathing.

✓ Make sure that you look right for the occasion – looking your best does wonders for your self-confidence. Try to avoid wearing anything for the first time – you will not feel comfortable and there may be problems, such as a jacket which is too tight when you reach up.

✓ Remember that the audience will be ready to respect and listen to what you have to say. They have come to hear and see you – a little self-belief and confidence in the value of what you are about to say will go a long way.

✗ Do not resort to alcohol – it will only slow you down and make you less responsive.

If your hands shake when you are nervous do not hold light sheets of paper – hold cards instead – no one will see your hands shaking then.

 "In a presentation to a large number of people, draw a letter 'M' over your audience with your eyes, moving up one side to the back, down to the middle and up towards the far right corner and back down the side to the front. That way you can cover most of audience without spending too long on any one part. This is especially useful when the auditorium is darkened, the lights are on you and it is difficult to see anyone beyond the first few rows."
Cristina Stuart, SpeakEasy Training

Prepare your voice

The more relaxed you feel, the more you are able to rely on your voice to project and sound confident. Nervousness is bound to make your throat feel dry – make sure that there is a glass of water within reach but don't drink iced water; this can tighten the throat, which won't help.

Prepare your voice by doing some exercises – rehearse your opening delivery, a favourite poem, even your address and telephone number. In other words, get your voice working before the presentation but don't strain it.

Some people find it useful to have a throat lozenge handy – but try not to be sucking on one as you give your introduction!

Making the presentation –

keeping on an even keel and handling the hiccups

"Many people lack enthusiasm in their presentation. They are often worried about appearing flippant or not being taken seriously. Unfortunately they box themselves into being seen as a stereotypical business person and don't use their personality. They need to loosen up a little bit and take themselves out of their strait-jacket and find ways of being less inhibited. Smile at the audience – it is not their fault that you are feeling nervous. They want to listen to a speaker who looks as if they are enjoying the occasion!"
Cristina Stuart, SpeakEasy Training

THE FIRST FEW MINUTES

Your priorities in the first few minutes are to introduce yourself, set the scene and relax your audience.

- As you approach the platform or front of the room, smile and make sure that your body language looks relaxed and confident (even if you aren't).

- Once you reach the platform (or if you are already there), pause before beginning the presentation. There is no rush. Relax – set the pace and, just for a moment, let the audience anticipate what your presentation will be like.

- Thank the person who introduced you in a warm and friendly way. Greet the audience.

Never sit behind a desk to give a presentation.

- If your audience is small, try to establish eye contact. Break the ice.

In an informal setting you can use an ice-breaking exercise such as asking the audience to find out as much as they can in one minute about the person sitting next to them or to find x things they have in common.

* Introduce yourself in a light, informal way (but keep it brief no life histories).

* Begin your introduction – the one you have learnt off by heart – while maintaining eye contact with the audience.

Watch anxious movements. Twitchy fingers and fidgety feet will only get in the way of what you have to say.

 "After a presentation many people say that towards the end of it they actually started to enjoy giving the presentation, whereas before the presentation it is the thing they are running away from most. If you can get that element of enjoyment in earlier rather than later, that is one of the the keys to success."
Cristina Stuart, SpeakEasy Training

HOW DO I KEEP THE PRESENTATION SMOOTH?

Use the notes written on the index cards you have prepared. Keep the relevant card in your palm do not keep going back to the desk to check your script.

Your rehearsals will have taught you how to keep the flow running smoothly between talk and visual aids.

In a large auditorium sweep the audience with your eyes so that each member feels that you are talking directly to him or her.

 "In a small presentation you must have eye contact with everyone. Watch out for those people closest you, especially if they are seated in the shape of a horseshoe. You might find that you tend to look at them less. Make sure that you haven't got any blind spots. Every member of the audience should get an equal amount of eye contact."
Cristina Stuart, SpeakEasy Training

HOW DO I DEAL WITH INTERRUPTIONS?

Most presenters at one time or another find that something or someone will interrupt their flow. If the disturbance is caused by external factors such as a sudden burst of drilling outside the window, an unscheduled arrival (for example, of the caterers) or any outside noise, follow the advice below:

1. Do not try to compete with the noise.
2. Keep calm and stay in control – apologise to the audience and talk to them in a light-hearted way to keep their attention (and to keep them on your side).
3. When you are ready to re-start, summarise what you have said so far (or go back to the previous visual aid) and continue.

Have a dry throat? Keep some water handy, but don't drink iced water – it will tighten, not loosen your vocal chords.

If someone in the audience interrupts you (assuming that you have not invited questions to be posed at any time):

1. Deal with the interrupter in a calm, positive and good-humoured way. Do not get annoyed.
2. Deal with any serious criticism or comment immediately – or say that you were coming to that very point or that you will deal with it in due course.
3. Say that you will deal with questions later, but thank the person for making the point.
4. Put up your next visual aid to signal that you want to move the presentation on.
5. Treat "funny" remarks in a light-hearted way – go with the joke (even if you hate it).

Remember that the key to interruptions is to keep the audience on your side, fully alert and ready to continue when you are allowed. Stay in control.

"If you want to regain your audience's attention back to the presentation, tell them that you want to review where you have got to and then you would like to ask some questions. Once an audience thinks it is going to be asked questions it will pay more attention to you."

Cristina Stuart, SpeakEasy Training

DYNAMIC DELIVERY

Here are some useful tips from experienced presenters on making sure that your vocal delivery is lively, interesting and dynamic.

Use variety in your voice

- Vary the pitch to make your voice sound interesting: vary between low and high (but not too high!).

- Change the volume – either a sudden increase or decrease can capture the audience's attention.

- Use short dramatic pauses of around three seconds to introduce an important idea or to signal that this is something the audience needs to think about.

- Vary the speed of delivery – sometimes slow and deliberate, other times quicker, more excited.

If the audience becomes involved in a discussion that seems to be going off the subject, put up the next transparency to pull the audience's attention back to you.

Hesitation

- Work on getting rid of hesitation – try to avoid too many "ers" and "you knows".

- If you are lost for words, relax and pause – the audience will never know.

- Avoid useless phrases that only serve to pad things out. Chief offenders here are:
  - ✗ "As I am sure many of you are aware..."
  - ✗ "It does not need me to tell you that..."
  - ✗ "It goes without saying that..."

- Be short, crisp and incisive.

"It is important to gain eye contact with individual people within your audience. You will usually find there is someone in the audience who is a real smiley-eye person. This gives me a boost because I know then that I have got an ally in the audience – somebody there who is wishing me to do well. That does your own confidence a power of good. Do remember to give other members of your audience eye contact as well. "
Catherine de Salvo, Fenman Training

Watch your language!

* Avoid using words that you wouldn't normally use in everyday conversation. The presentation should not sound like a written statement. Be yourself, as if you were talking to a small group of trusted colleagues.

* Keep your tone friendly, unpompous and above all personal. For example:
    * ✗ The purchase of comestibles, it is believed, is dependent upon the consumers' knowledge of market conditions.
    * ✓ It's price and quality that make a customer buy.

Avoid abstract nouns

Abstract nouns are much beloved of some presenters who like to put up slides that read like a lexicon of such words. For instance:

intelligence
idealism
inspiration
integration
individualism
intuition

Such lists are fairly sterile and mean little to an audience trying to catch the main points of your presentation.

Treat the audience as one person

Talk to the audience as though it were one person – you will sound much more approachable and interesting to everyone concerned.

Mannerisms

* Don't be tempted to resort to gestures or mannerisms that are unnatural to you – like using your hands when you speak or shaking your head. Be natural and be yourself!

* Avoid distracting mannerisms:
    * ✗ adjusting your clothing as you speak;
    * ✗ scratching your ear or nose;
    * ✗ brushing back your hair;
    * ✗ flicking off real or imaginary dust.

Everyone has their own often endearing mannerisms, but overuse can distract the audience.

To be able to persuade your audience you need to understand what they agree with, what they disagree with and what they are indifferent to. Make sure you appeal to their minds and emotions, don't expect facts and a logical argument to win the day.

HOW DO I COME TO A STRONG FINISH?

Here are some useful tips for rounding off your presentation in a confident and up-beat way. This is what experienced presenters advise:

- Finish on a high note – say something that looks forward, is optimistic or leaves the audience feeling enthused and ready for action.

- Avoid false endings such as "And finally..." when in fact you mean to go on for another 20 minutes.

- Thank the audience, the chairperson and anyone else who has helped you.

- Leave centre stage calmly and with a smile, looking forward to your next successful presentation.

 "Aim to give handouts at the end unless the audience needs them to follow the presentation."
Cristina Stuart, SpeakEasy Training

We've had a rough time of it lately ...

... the future looks brighter

MAKING A PRESENTATION IN A HURRY

Most people have been in the situation where they have had to make a presentation with little time to prepare. If you get a call to make a presentation in, say, two days or less – don't panic! Here are some tips for making an effective presentation when there is little time to get ready.

We will assume that you don't have any materials prepared although it is always possible to adapt what you have used in the past.

1. Use OHP transparencies and a flipchart.

2. Spend no more than two hours deciding what you need to say:
    * Write down as many points as you can think of – don't worry about getting them in order or sifting out unimportant things at this stage;
    * Go through your notes:
        – tick those points which are essential and put a cross against any which are important;
        – cross out any ideas which may be desirable but are neither important nor essential.
    * Now make some order out of your notes:
        – which points are to be given in your introduction?
        – which points should be in your main section?
        – which points belong in your conclusion?

3. Prepare no more than one transparency for each five-minute period of your presentation. If, for instance, the presentation is due to last for 25 minutes, prepare five transparencies.

 "When you have very little time to prepare a presentation, it's amazing how easy it is to do too much."
Chief executive of a food manufacturer

4. Use the transparencies to illustrate key points in your talk:
    ☐ key points to remember;
    ☐ essential data to note: facts and figures, trends, results, growth figures, proportions, time comparisons and so on;
    ☐ simplifying charts that will help the audience to understand and remember what you are saying – flow charts are especially useful to show how one thing is related to another.

5. If you are confident in their use, create text and graphics using your word processor and presentation software.

6. Try to include at least one colourful transparency that will look professional. If you can only produce one, make it the last transparency you show – it will leave a good impression on the audience.

7. Get a flipchart, easel and pens ready for any discussion points. You could always decide to use just the flipchart to make your key points. This is perfectly feasible where the audience is fairly small, say under 20 people.

8. Half an hour before the presentation (or sooner if you have time):
    ☐ check the room;
    ☐ check the equipment.

Remember ... keep calm and stay in control.

Over half the impact you make on an audience is through what they see. Under 40 per cent is due to the tone and intonation of the speaker and just over 5 per cent with the actual words that are said. Get the visual impact right and you are half way there to winning the battle.

Appendix **I**

Rapid reference presentation planner

What to do when you are asked to make a presentation

Decide in general terms what you are going to say. 1	Write out a rough script – then reduce it down to just what is essential, and what is desirable if you have time. 2	Choose which visual aids you are going to use: • Flipchart • Whiteboard • OHP • 35mm slides • Video 3
Prepare your visual aids. 4	Choose the venue (if this is down to you). 5	

At least one week before

Rehearse your presentation several times, with the visual aids. 1	Time your presentation carefully. 2	Decide if there is anything you need to leave out. 3
Get some feedback from someone you trust 4	Act on their recommendations and make appropriate changes. 5	

1–2 days before

Have a final rehearsal, if possible in the actual venue. 1	If you have a choice, decide how you are going to arrange the room. 2	Prepare any remaining visual aids. 3

On the day

Be aware of the main news events and if any relate to your presentation. 1	Arrive at the venue with at least an hour to spare. 2	Check the room layout. 3
Check that all the equipment is working and test focus your transparencies and slides. 4	Check that you can be seen and heard from the back. 5	

30 minutes before

Get yourself mentally and physically prepared. 1	Do some relaxation exercises. 2	Prepare your voice. 3

5 minutes before

Run through your opening remarks. 1	Approach your presentation positively and confidently. 2	Remember to smile and look at your audience 3

Appendix **II**

Presentation problem buster

FLIPCHARTS	
Do you want to write notes on a flipchart?	Use light pencil or a yellow marker which will not be seen by the audience.
Do you want to keep several key points in front of the group?	Pin or stick completed flipchart sheets around the room.
Do you want to emphasise key words on a flipchart?	Draw boxes around them.
Do you want to keep bullets and margins in line on a flipchart?	Use a pad with squared paper.
Do you want to keep columns of figures straight on a flipchart?	Draw column rules in pencil in advance, or use squared paper.
Do you want to use a complicated graphic in a flipchart presentation, such as a series of boxes or a flow chart?	Draw the outline beforehand in faint pencil, or in thick marker pen on the sheet behind the one you will be writing on.
Do you want people at the back of the room to read your flipchart?	Use lettering 15–20mm high.
Do you want people at the back to read the whole of your flipchart page?	Leave a bigger margin at the bottom than at the top.
Do you want to avoid obscuring the chart as you write on it?	Stand to the right of the chart with the audience on your left if you are right-handed (and vice versa if you are left-handed).
Do you want to store flipchart sheets?	Fasten them together at the top with bulldog clips, roll them up and hold the roll together with strong elastic bands.

WHITEBOARDS	
Does your whiteboard look grimy?	Clean it with an alcohol-based cleaner.
Do you want to keep your writing straight on a whiteboard or flipchart?	Draw guidelines in faint yellow marker before the presentation.
Do you want to write in a straight line without using pre-drawn rules?	Move your writing hand by using all your arm and not just your wrist.
Do you want to distinguish between two sets of ideas on a whiteboard or flipchart?	Use a different colour for each set.
Do you want to make something stand out on a whiteboard?	Use a fluorescent marker.
Do you want to use an overhead projector but do not have a screen?	Try projecting onto a whiteboard if there is one available.
OVERHEAD PROJECTORS	
Do you want to write directly on transparencies?	Use a film made from acetate or hard PVC.
Do you want to produce transparencies via a photocopier or computer?	Use a film made from polyester.
Do you want to turn a graphic or drawing into a transparency?	Copy it onto OHP film using a photocopier.
Do you want to produce high quality colour transparencies?	Use a thermal transfer printer.
Do you want to write on transparencies and use them repeatedly?	Use permanent OHP markers.
Do you need to erase ink from a permanent marker on a transparency?	Use a special correction pen.
Do you want to use a highlighter on top of other text on a transparency?	Work on the reverse side of the film to avoid smudging.

Do you want to underline words on a transparency with a ruler?	A fine-tipped marker is less likely to bleed under the edge of the ruler.
Do you have difficulty keeping your handwriting straight on a transparency?	Use a lined or grid backing sheet.
Do you need to draw a complicated illustration on a transparency?	Draw it in pencil on the backing sheet first, lay the transparency over and trace with an OHP marker.
Do you want your audience to see your transparency?	Use lettering at least 8mm in height.
Do you want your transparency to be read easily?	Make sure there are no more than seven words to a line.
Do you want your transparency to look uncluttered?	Make sure there are no more than ten lines to a page, and ideally seven.
Has your text been typed on a typewriter or wordprocessor?	Use the enlarge facility on a photocopier to increase the size of the lettering and copy this onto a transparency.
Do you want typed text to be easy to read?	Use a sans serif typeface such as Helvetica or Univers.
Do you want to make your graphics stand out on a transparency?	Use red or orange marker pens.
Do you want to make an image recede on a transparency?	Use blue marker pen.
Do you want to write crib notes on a transparency?	Write them with a fine-tipped yellow marker which won't be seen from the audience.
Do you want to make a long OHP presentation more restful to watch?	Use colour-tinted transparencies.
Do you want to make a clear separation between different parts of an OHP presentation?	Use a different colour of transparency for each section.

Do you want to colour in areas of a pie chart or histogram on a transparency?	Use broad-tipped coloured markers or self-adhesive coloured film.
Do you want to add cartoons or graphics to a transparency?	Buy or borrow books of clip art.
Is your handwriting difficult to read?	If you do not have access to a wordprocessor, use dry transfer lettering or stencils.
Are you unsure of your ability to design an effective transparency?	Some presentation software incorporates templates which design the layout for you.
Do you want to keep your transparencies in order?	Number each with a light yellow marker.
Do you want to keep your transparencies in a ring binder?	Use transparent sleeves or card mounts.
Do you want to avoid your transparencies curling in the heat?	Mount them in a card frame or Flip-Frame™.
Would you like to use several transparencies in quick succession?	Consider a film roll rather than sheets.
35mm SLIDES	
Do you want to stop 35mm slides falling out of a carousel in transit?	Seal the carousel with tape.
Do you want to avoid your audience looking at a glaring screen?	Have blank slides ready to insert between the slides you want to show.
Do you want to keep your slides in order?	Number them on the frame in order of presentation.
VIDEO	
Do you want to show a video to a group of more than 20 people?	Use a video projector or a number of TV monitors.
Do you want to be able to find your place in a video?	Use a video player with a counter and number all your cues.

PRESENTATION TECHNIQUES	
Do you want your message to be clear?	List the essential points in order of priority and make sure they appear in your presentation.
Do you need to present complex information?	Use an appropriate visual aid – a graph, flow chart or illustration.
Do you want to get across a series of ideas which builds into a larger picture?	Use an overlay technique with OHP transparencies.
Are you unable to decide what to include in your presentation?	Divide your notes into three categories: essential, desirable and unnecessary.
Does your text seem dull?	Attract attention by beginning each line with a noun or an active verb.
Do you need to present lots of figures?	A graph, chart or drawing is more interesting than a table of figures.
Do you have to present a complex flow chart?	A series of charts or an overlay technique may be clearer.
Do your figures represent trends over time?	Display them as a bar chart or histogram.
Do your figures represent a relationship between two or more variables?	Display them as a graph.
Do you want to illustrate a sequential process?	Display it as a flow chart.
Do you want to add topical interest to your presentation?	Make sure you are aware of events in the news that day.
Do you need to overcome nervousness?	Rehearse your presentation thoroughly.
Do you keep losing track?	Write key words on a prompt card.
Do you need notes but don't want to use prompt cards?	Write pencil notes on the card mounts of your transparencies.

Are you concerned about keeping to time?	Keep your watch within view.
Do you want to minimise last-minute stress?	Get to the venue with at least an hour to spare.
Does your throat feel dry when you are nervous?	Make sure there is a glass of water within reach.
Do you want to prepare your voice?	Recite a favourite poem or your address and telephone number.
Does your voice sound uninteresting?	Vary the pitch, change the volume, or use short dramatic pauses.
Do you want to move the presentation on after a question from the audience?	Put up the next slide or transparency or write something on the flipchart.
Do you want to stimulate discussion in a small group?	Try a circle or cafeteria layout.
Do you want to give your presentation a formal feel?	Arrange seating in theatre style.
Do you want your visual aids to look professional?	Develop a clear house style keep colours, designs, typefaces and font sizes consistent.

Index

A abbreviations 76
abstract nouns 145
acetate 24, 29
audience
   declining attention 25
   eye contact with *see* eye contact
   'hooking' 117
   inattentive 128
   involving 12, 18, 90, 116, 126
   nature of 117
   prior knowledge 117–8
   regaining attention with questions 143
   researching 137
   size 118–9
   test audience 135
   treating as one person 145

B bar charts 44, 84–5
   3-D 85
board copiers 96
boxes (for text) 76–7
breaking the ice 125, 141–2
bubblejet printers 26
built-in screens, small 101
bullet points 81–2

C cafeteria layout 62, 63
card mounts 58
carousel loading systems 99, 104
charts
   flipcharts 84–5
   OHP transparencies 43–49
   see also graphics
circle presentation 60, 61
clip art 40–1
colour

flipcharts 81, 90
OHP transparencies 38–40
slides 103
whiteboard 94, 97
colour combinations 39–40, 102
coloured film 25, 39
   self-adhesive 48
complex information 4, 117
computers 22, 53–57
   computer images projected onto OHP
      screen 55–57
   graphics 55
   presentation software 54–5
   printers 25–7
   word processors 53–4
copyboard 95–6

D delivery, dynamic 144–6
Deltascreen 101
desktop screens 101
dot matrix printers 26
dress rehearsal 136
dry transfer lettering 50

E easel, flipchart 10
electronic copyboards 95
ending the presentation 146
eye contact
   importance of 36, 129, 142, 174
   OHP 12

F feedback 135
figures *see* numbers/figures
film
   OHP *see* overhead projector film
   video compared with 21

finishing the presentation 146
flipchart 6, 22, 73–92
    advantages and disadvantages 10–12
    audience size and 119
    design of effective sheets 76–87
        bullet points 81–2
        clarity and visibility 80–1
        colour 81, 90
        design techniques 82–7
        text 76–81
    enhancing the use of 90
    equipment 74
    preparation checklist 91–2
    presentations at short notice 147
    problem buster 151
    prompts 76, 130
    reveal technique 87–90
    room 73
    troubleshooting 91
flipchart easel 10
flipchart pads 74–5
Flip-Frame 58, 138
flow charts 45, 86
fluorescent colours 94, 97
font (typeface) 33–4

G graphics/visuals
    clip art 40–1
    flipchart 83
    graphics guides 50
    OHP transparencies 36, 39, 40–49, 50, 55
    presentation of figures 43–49
    presentation software 55
    transfer graphics 50
graphs 43–5, 85
    see also charts

H handouts 12, 34, 104, 146
hands, presenter's 118, 140
hecklers 7
    see also interruptions
hesitation 144
highlighters 28–9
histograms see bar charts

horseshoe presentation 60, 61
humour 129, 133

I ice-breaking 125, 141–2
information
    complex 4, 117
        types given in presentations 7
inkjet printers 26
interruptions, dealing with 143
    see also hecklers

K key words/phrases 82
keystone effect 101
KISS (keep it short and simple) 130

L landscape format 31
language 145
laser printers 26
LCD (liquid crystal display) projection
        panels 56–7
length of presentation 120–1, 122
lettering see text/lettering
lightboxes 100, 104
lighting 119
    slide projection 105
line graphs 43
lines per page/sheet
    flipcharts 77, 78, 79
    OHP 32, 33

M making the presentation 141–8
    beginning 141–2
    calmness and control 148
    dealing with interruptions 143
    dynamic delivery 144–6
    with short notice 146–7
    smooth flow 142
    strong ending 146
mannerisms 147
markers/pens 67
    OHP transparencies 27–9
    tip widths 28, 94
    whiteboard 94–5
materials 125–33

adding variety 130–1
deciding what to use 127
elements of a good story 128–9
KISS (keep it short and simple) 130
outline 125–9
prompts 129–30
seamless presentation with visual
    aids 131–2
message 116–7

N narrative 128
non-permanent OHP markers 27
notes *see* outline
numbers/figures 103
flipcharts 86
OHP transparencies 41–49

O opening the presentation 121
outline 123–9
deciding what to use 127
framework for writing 126
story 128–9
overhead projector (OHP) 22, 24–74
advantages and disadvantages 12–16
audience size 119
best use of projector 66–68
care of projector 59
checklist for effective use 70–1
computers and *see* computers
equipment 23
overlay technique 51–3
pens and markers 27–9
preparation 65–6
preparation of room 59–65
presentations at short notice 147
prompts 130, 132
reveal technique 68–70
overhead projector (OHP) film 24
rolls 24–5
overhead projector (OHP) screens
positioning 64–5
overhead projector (OHP) transparencies
see transparencies
overlay technique 51–3

P pen plotters 27, 90
pens *see* markers/pens
permanent markers
cleaning whiteboards 95
OHP 27–8
personal experience 128
photocopiers 24, 25, 71
pie charts 46–9
planning the presentation 115–123
audience 117
    prior knowledge 117–8
    size 118–9
checklist 123
desired result 121–3
length of presentation 120–1
message 116–7
starting the presentation 121
venue 120
pointers 90
portable screens 101
portrait format 31
positioning
OHP screens 64–5
video 109
preparation 133–40
dress rehearsal 136
feedback 135
flipchart 91–2
OHP 65–6
for presentations at short notice 146–7
rehearsals 134
relaxation immediately beforehand 139
slide projection 104
technical problems 138–9
video 108, 110
voice 140
whiteboard 97–8
presentation software 54–5
see also computers
printers, computer 25–7
proactive group sessions 11
projection panels, LCD 56–7
projectors *see* overhead projector; slide

projection
prompt cards 129
prompts 10, 129
purpose of presentation 121–3

Q questions
regaining audience's attention 143
tricky 133

R rapid reference planner 149–50
rehearsals 5, 100, 134, 137
dress rehearsal 136
relaxation 139
result of presentation, desired 121–3
reveal technique
flipchart 87–9
OHP 68–70
room/venue
flipchart 73
OHP 59–65
preparation checklist 120
whiteboard 97
rotary carousels 100

S sans serif fonts 33–4
screens
OHP *see* overhead projector screen
35 mm slides 101–2
scripts 129
seating layout 60–4
self-adhesive coloured film 48–9
shallow V presentation 62
slide projection 22, 99–105
advantages and disadvantages 19–20
audience size 119
checklist of tips 105
equipment 99–102
projectors 119–101
screens 101–2
exciting visuals 102
lighting 105
preparation 104
see also 35 mm slides
slide show, computer-created 56–7

software, presentation 54–5
see also computers
starting the presentation 121
storage
OHP transparencies 57–9
35 mm slides 103
whiteboard information 95–6
story 128–9
structure of presentation 128

T technical problems 138–9
templates 54–5
test audience 135
text/lettering
dry transfer lettering 50
flipchart 76–81
OHP 30–5
size 30, 77, 97
35 mm slides 102
typed 33–4
upper and lower case 33, 80, 96
whiteboard 96
theatre-style seating 62–3
thermal transfer printers 27
35 mm slides 7, 22
producing own 103
storage 103
see also slide projection
timing of presentation 120–1, 122
transfer lettering/graphics 50
transparencies, OHP 7
accessories for professional appearance 50
computer printers and 25–7
creating effective transparencies 37–42
colour 38–40
film rolls 24–5
graphics 36, 39, 40–1, 50, 55
materials made from 24
overlay technique 51–3
photocopier-produced 25
preparation 29–37
by hand 29–33
use of space 35–7

presenting numbers 43–9
storage and preservation 57–9
text 30–4
see also overhead projector
transparent sleeves 58
tripod screens 101
typed text 33–4
typeface 33–4

V variety
adding 130–1
vocal 144
venue *see* room/venue
video 22, 107–11
advantages and disadvantages 21
equipment 107
finding one's place 111
making the most of 110–1
positioning monitors/screens 109
preparation 108, 110, 111
problem buster 154
visibility
flipchart 80–1
whiteboard 97
visual aids 3–22
achieving seamless presentation 131–2
deciding what to use 127
feeling comfortable with 8

getting the most from 9
and information to be presented 7–8
need to use 3–5
pitfalls 4–5
selection 22
technical problems 138–9
types available 6–7
see also under individual names
voice
audibility 138
preparation 140
and slide projection 103
variety in 144

W wall-mounted screens 101
white space 35–6, 83
whiteboard 22, 93–98
advantages and disadvantages 16–9
audience size 119
cleaning 94–5
colour 94, 97
equipment 93–4
keeping information 95–6
preparation for presentation 97–8
problem buster 152
text 96–7
wordprocessors 53–4
words per line 32

Free Special Report

(published price £14.95)

Which one would you like?

- ❑ Dirty Negotiating Tactics and their Solutions
- ❑ Organise Yourself to be Lazy
- ❑ Clear Your Desk Once and For All
- ❑ How to Bankrupt a Rogue Company
- ❑ Achieving ISO9000 – How much will it cost?
- ❑ Finding and Bidding for Bargain Properties at Auction

We would like to send you the Free Special Report of your choice.

Why?

Because we would like to add you name to our Business Enquirers Group – a selection of business people who receive regular information from us. We will offer you the best and most practical business books published, newsletters, a book review and also offers from other companies with products and services that may interest you.

To order your free report and join the Business Enquirers Group, simply phone, fax or write, give us your name, job title, address, phone, fax and e-mail numbers (if available) and quote MM02. And don't forget to tell us which report you want!

☏ 01353 665544

Ask for your free report by title and remember to quote our reference MM02

Fax 01353 667666

Photocopy this page, complete this box and fax it through to us

Name ———————————— Job title ————————————	
Company ————————————————————————	
Address ————————————————————————	
———————————— Postcode ————————————	
Phone ———————— Fax ———————— e-mail ————————	

Post

Wyvern Business Library MM02, FREEPOST CB511, Ely, Cambs CB7 4BR

Photocopy this page, fill in the box above (or staple your business card to it) and send it to us (no stamp required).